Asa Hull

Songs of praise and delight

A collection of original and selected songs for Sunday schools and young people's

meetings

Asa Hull

Songs of praise and delight
A collection of original and selected songs for Sunday schools and young people's meetings

ISBN/EAN: 9783337270445

Printed in Europe, USA, Canada, Australia, Japan

Cover: Foto ©Thomas Meinert / pixelio.de

More available books at **www.hansebooks.com**

SONGS OF
PRAISE AND DELIGHT.

A COLLECTION OF

ORIGINAL AND SELECTED SONGS

FOR

Sunday Schools and
Young People's Meetings.

EDITED BY

ASA HULL,

AUTHOR AND PUBLISHER OF SUNDAY SCHOOL MUSIC BOOKS, PROGRAMMES FOR CHRISTMAS,
EASTER, CHILDREN'S DAY, HARVEST HOME AND THANKSGIVING, ETC.

———→×←———

NEW YORK:
Published by ASA HULL, 132 Nassau Street.

FOR SALE BY MUSIC DEALERS AND BOOKSELLERS GENERALLY.

COPYRIGHT, 1898, BY ASA HULL.

PREFACE.

SONGS OF PRAISE AND DELIGHT is the result of many years experience and observation, and is the embodiment of our ideas as to what the Sunday School and its auxiliary Societies need. From the large range of high grade music at our command, only the best adapted to this purpose has been selected; nothing has been admitted that is not of a high order, either words or music.

It is too often the case that a few pieces are sung over and over until they are worn out, and then the book is laid aside and many of the best songs never are used. There is not a dull tune in the book, but some pieces will appear more attractive than others on the first trial, but if thoroughly learned they will be found to be real gems. Such pieces as "The Armor of God," "The Christian Soldier," "Crown Him Forever," "Ye Soldiers of the Lord, Arise," "The Sacred Stream," "Fair Galilee," "Excelsior," "Marching to the Land Above," "The Battle March," and many others of that class are worthy of special attention.

Much must be left to the taste of the musical conductor, but we suggest that songs with only one part arranged as solos, may be sung by all in unison; never discard a good song because it is not convenient to use it as a solo. On the other hand songs having full harmony parts may be sung as solos, and it makes a pleasing variety to have those with a Refrain sung as Solo and Chorus, all singing the Refrain.

It is customary to sing the Chorus after each stanza, but if that makes the piece too lengthy the Chorus may be sung only after the closing verse. In some cases it might be considered advisable to omit the Chorus altogether.

With these suggestions "*Songs of Praise and Delight*" is prayerfully submitted for the generous consideration of all lovers of good Sunday School Music.

THE AUTHOR.

SPECIAL NOTICE. Nearly every piece in this book is copyright property, and all rights to print or reprint its contents, or any part thereof, are reserved exclusively to the proprietor of the same.

ASA HULL'S MUSIC TYPOGRAPHY.

SONGS of PRAISE AND DELIGHT.

CROWNED WITH PRAISE.

R. L. FLETCHER.   Copyright, 1898, by Asa Hull.   ASA HULL.

1. With our praise we'll crown the Saviour, With thanksgiving we'll re-joice;
2. In life's ra-diant morn we'll serve Him, And will strive His works to do,
3. Since it was for us He suf-fered, Dy-ing on the accursed tree,
4. Yes, for all the gifts He brings us, And for all His pa-tient love,

For His love to us so pre-cious, We will lift our grateful voice.
Giv - ing Him our best en - deav-or, Who will keep us ev - er true.
That for ev - er, we His child-ren, Might from sin and death be free.
We will serve Him here with gladness, And will sing His praise a - bove.

CHORUS.

We will praise Him, we will praise Him Whom the an - gel hosts a - dore;

With a pure heart we will praise Him, And we'll praise Him ev - er - more!

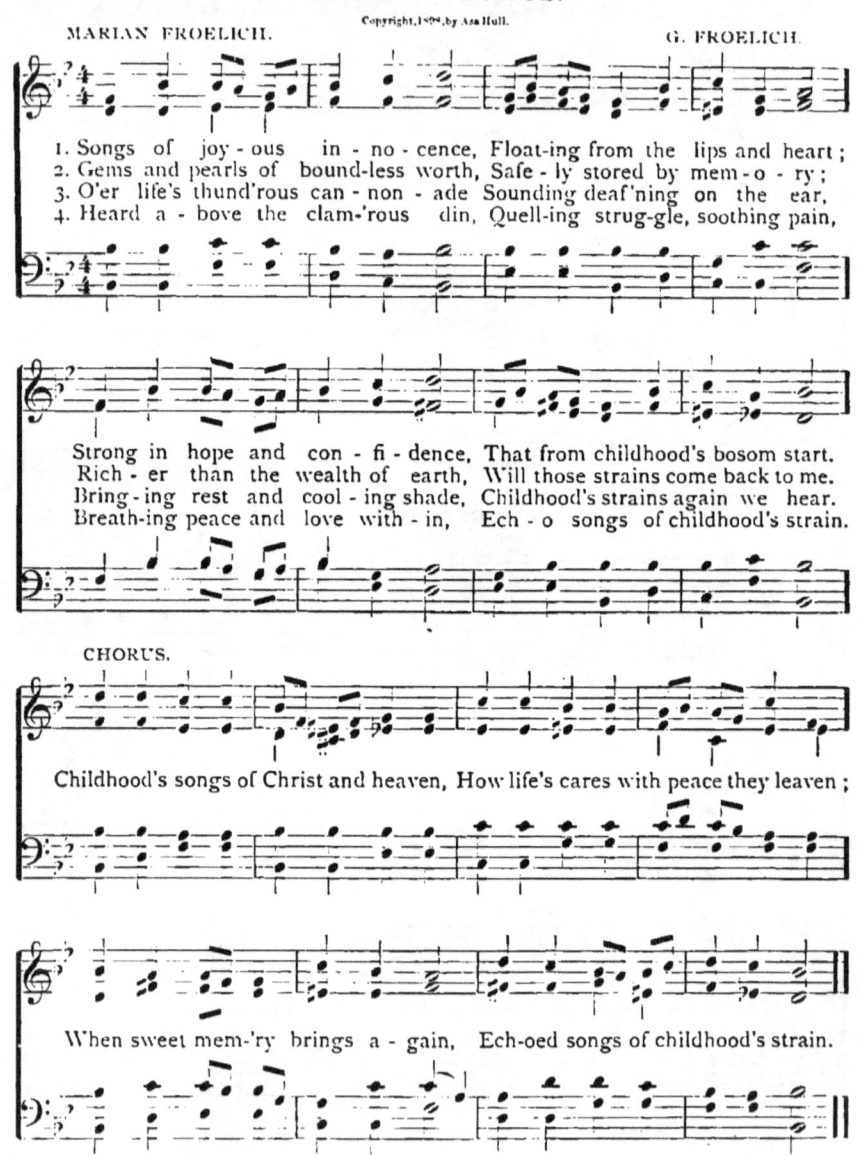

WAVES OF LOVE.

REV. R. W. TODD.   Copyright, 1898, by Asa Hull.   ASA HULL.

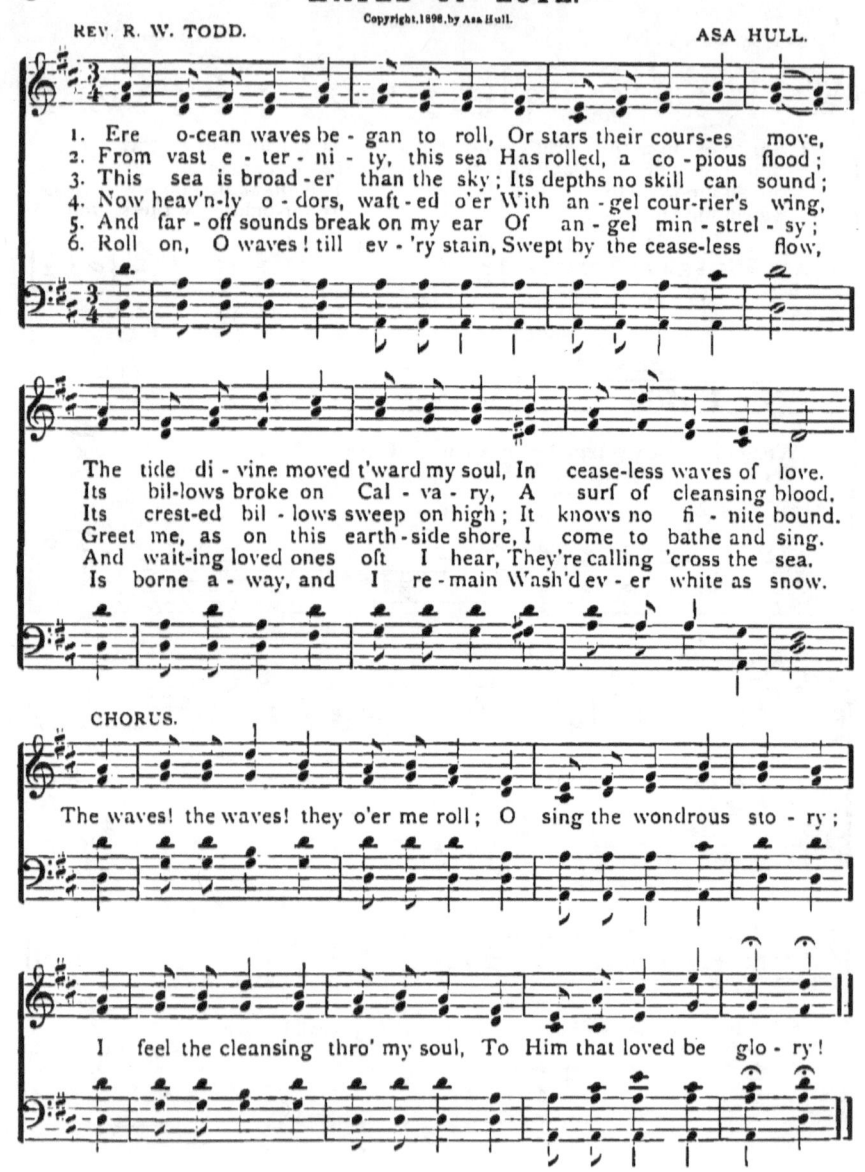

1. Ere o-cean waves be-gan to roll, Or stars their cours-es move,
2. From vast e-ter-ni-ty, this sea Has rolled, a co-pious flood;
3. This sea is broad-er than the sky; Its depths no skill can sound;
4. Now heav'n-ly o-dors, waft-ed o'er With an-gel cour-rier's wing,
5. And far-off sounds break on my ear Of an-gel min-strel-sy;
6. Roll on, O waves! till ev-'ry stain, Swept by the cease-less flow,

The tide di-vine moved t'ward my soul, In cease-less waves of love.
Its bil-lows broke on Cal-va-ry, A surf of cleansing blood.
Its crest-ed bil-lows sweep on high; It knows no fi-nite bound.
Greet me, as on this earth-side shore, I come to bathe and sing.
And wait-ing loved ones oft I hear, They're calling 'cross the sea.
Is borne a-way, and I re-main Wash'd ev-er white as snow.

CHORUS.

The waves! the waves! they o'er me roll; O sing the wondrous sto-ry;
I feel the cleansing thro' my soul, To Him that loved be glo-ry!

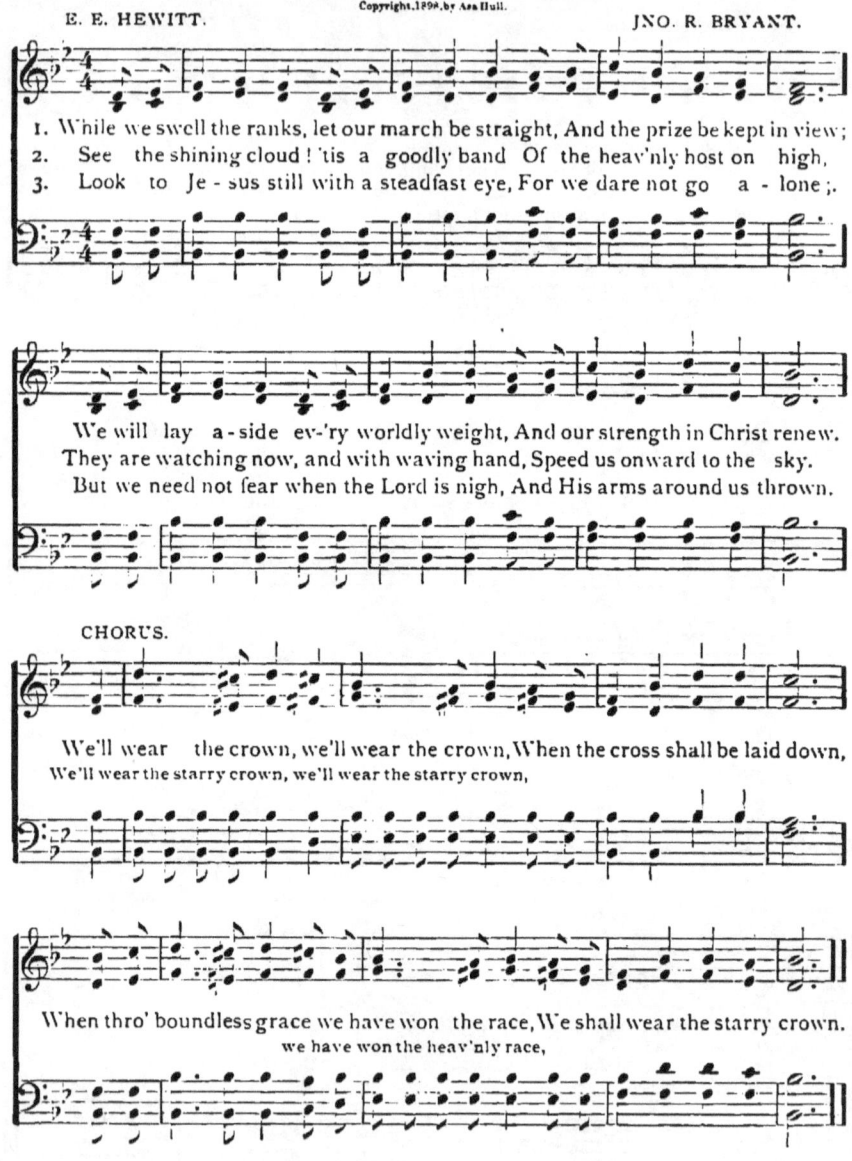

I AM GOING TO BE CROWNED—Concluded.

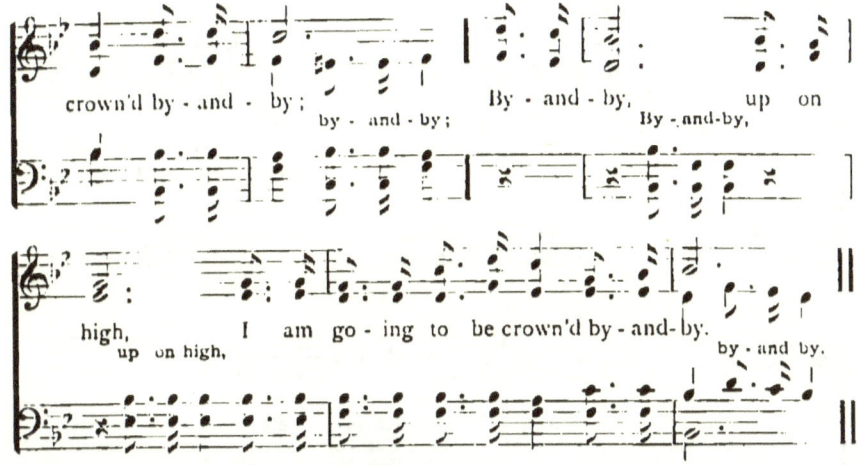

IN GLADNESS WE COME.

J. H. MOHLER.   Copyright, 1893, by Asa Hull.   J. H. ROSECRANS.

3 Thy children, Lord, have come,
   Up to Thy house of prayer;
   To praise Thy name in grateful song,
   Lord, bless Thy people there.

4 Thy peace in plenty give
   To all Thy children here;
   And prosper those Thy words receive,
   Thy holy name revere.

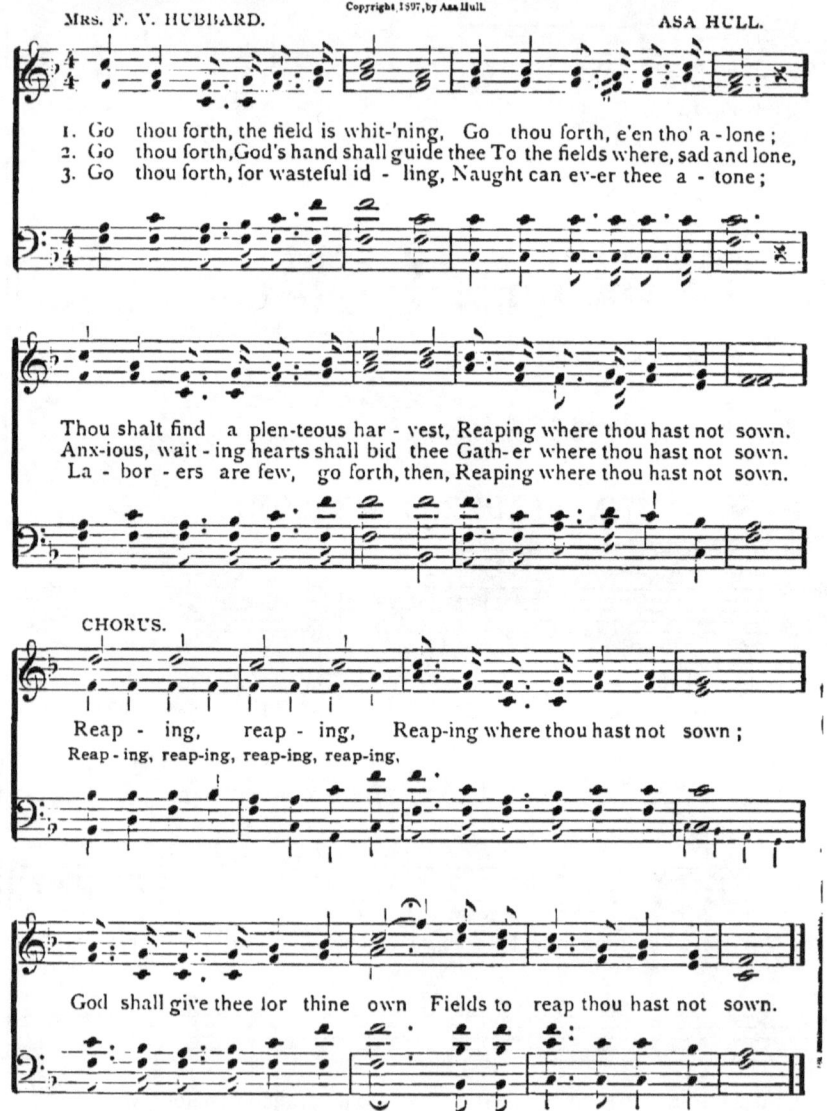

LET THE LIGHT SHINE IN.

E. R. LATTA.
Copyright, 1890, by Asa Hull.
J. E. HALL.

1. Is your spir-it dark with the clouds of doubt? Let the light shine in!
2. Is your soul bedimmed by the gloom of fear? Let the light shine in!
3. When your heart is bow'd with a load of care, Let the light shine in!
4. Ev-'ry day and hour to the end of strife, Let the light shine in!

At the Saviour's word they'll be driv-en out, Let the light shine in!
Just a look of love from the Lord will cheer, Let the light shine in!
There's a promis'd grace, it is yours to share, Let the light shine in!
Then, thro'-out the length of an end-less life, Shall the light shine in!

CHORUS.

Let the light, let the light, Let the light of love shine in!
Let the light, let the light, shine in!

Let the light, let the light, Let the light of love shine in!
Let the light, let the light, shine in!

GATHERING HOME—Concluded.

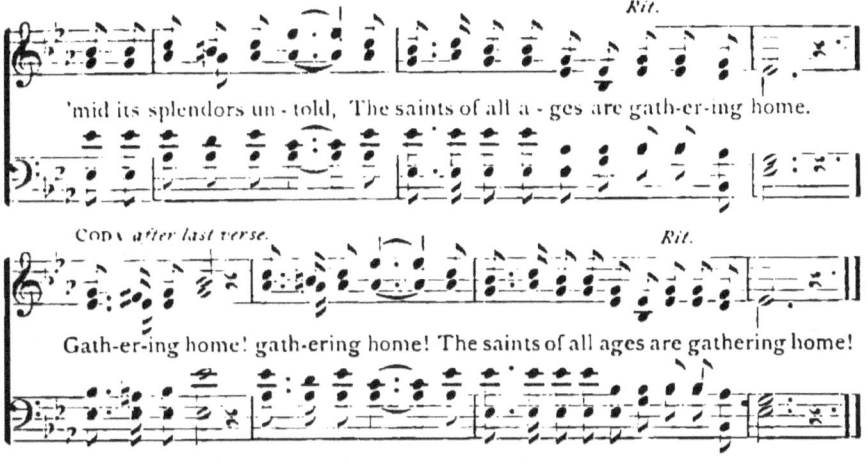

HOUR OF PRAYER.

PHŒBE H. BROWN. ASA HULL.

Copyright,1898,by Asa Hull.

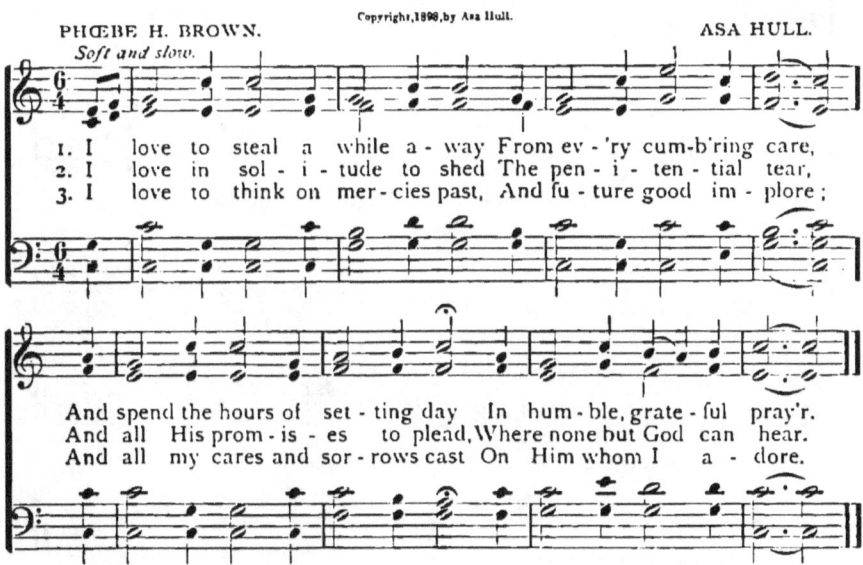

1. I love to steal a while a-way From ev-'ry cum-b'ring care,
And spend the hours of set-ting day In hum-ble, grate-ful pray'r.

2. I love in sol-i-tude to shed The pen-i-ten-tial tear,
And all His prom-is-es to plead, Where none but God can hear.

3. I love to think on mer-cies past, And fu-ture good im-plore;
And all my cares and sor-rows cast On Him whom I a-dore.

4 I love by faith to take a view
  Of brighter scenes in heaven:
  The prospect doth my strength renew,
  While here by tempest driven.

5 Thus, when life's toilsome day is o'er,
  May its departing ray
  Be calm as this impressive hour,
  And lead to endless day.

OH, BE READY—Concluded.

By-and-by we shall hear the midnight cry; Oh, be ready when the Bridegroom comes.

HIDE ME, SAVIOUR.

FRANK M. DAVIS.   Copyright, 1891, by Asa Hull.   FRANK M. DAVIS.

1. Hide me, O my Saviour, hide me 'Neath the shadow of Thy wing;
   When the tempest high is rag-ing, Let me there in safe-ty [OMIT] cling!

CHORUS.

Hide me, hide me, O my bless-ed Sav-iour, hide me;
Hide me, O my Saviour, Hide me, O my Saviour,

Hide me, hide me 'Neath the shadow of Thy wing!
Hide me, O my Saviour, Hide me, O my Saviour,   of Thy wing!

2 Hide me, O my Saviour, hide me,
   Save me from the tempter's pow'r;
   Let me feel Thy sacred presence
   With me every blessed hour!

3 Hide me, O my Saviour, hide me,
   Till the night of earth is past;
   Till I reach that quiet haven,
   Where my soul will rest at last!

SUNBEAMS.

S. P. C. By permission. S. P. CREASINGER.

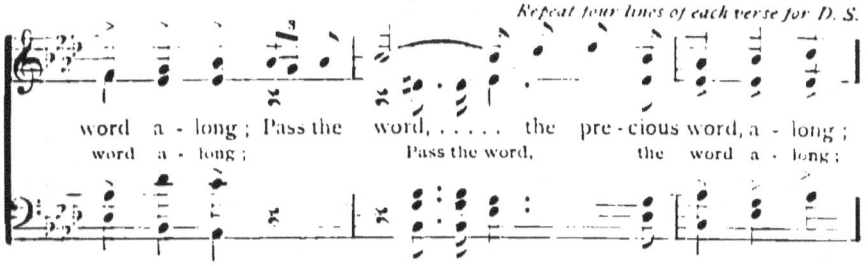

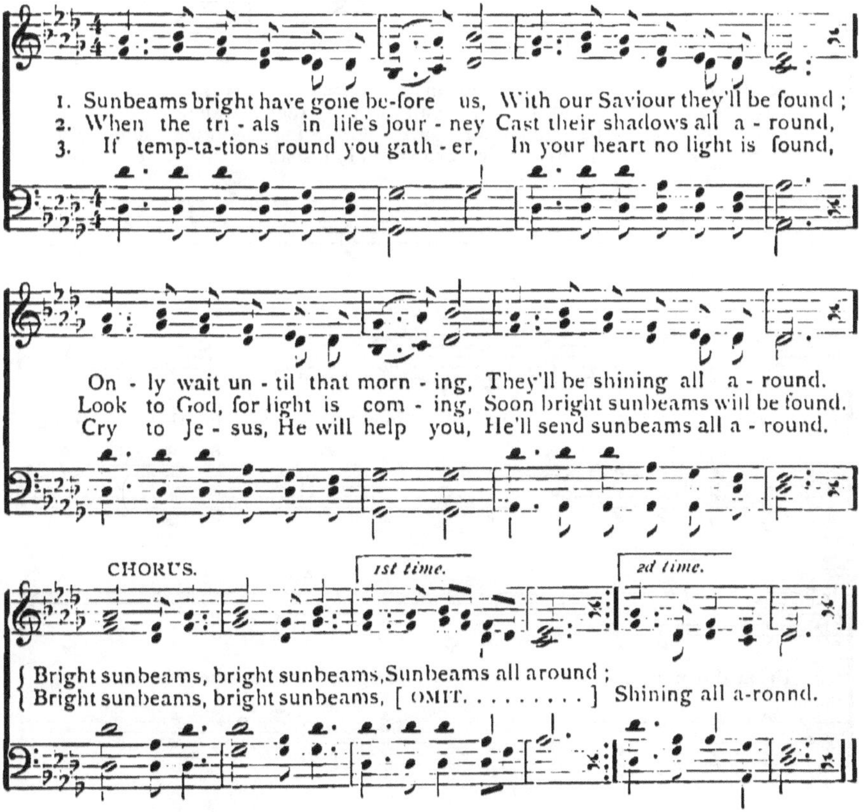

WHAT WILL THEY TELL JESUS?

REV. J. OATMAN, JR.
Copyright, 1895, by Asa Hull
ASA HULL.

1. Come, sin-ner, to Je-sus, oh, do not re-fuse, He's merciful, lov-ing and true;
2. The an-gels are camping about God's elect, And guarding them all the way thro';
3. These seasons so precious will soon pass from sight, The river of death you will view;

While an-gels to glo-ry are bearing the news, What will they tell Jesus for you?
You now have the choice to accept or re-ject, What will they tell Jesus for you?
Come, start with God's people for heaven to-night, What will they tell Jesus for you?

CHORUS.

What will they tell Jesus, those angels so bright? They wait to see what you will do;

While others are seeking the Saviour to-night, What will they tell Jesus for you?

'NEATH THE BANNER—Concluded.

We shall be vic-to-ri-ous, For our God is with the right.
We shall be, shall be vic-to-ri-ous,

THIS IS THE DAY.

E. R. LATTA.   Copyright, 1898, by Asa Hull.   ASA HULL.

1. Would you hear sal-va-tion's sto-ry ? This is the day !
   Would you seek a home in glo-ry ? [OMIT......]   This is the day !
2. Would you know your lost condition ? This is the day !
   Would you have the Great Physician ? [OMIT.....]   This is the day !
3. Would you start ere youth forsakes you ? This is the day !
   And be-fore old age o'ertakes you ? [OMIT......]   This is the day !

mf Let the Ho-ly Spir-it lead you, Let each hin-drance on-ly speed you,
Hast-en to the Fount of heal-ing, Hear the in-vi-ta-tion peal-ing,
Be not found with id-lers standing, But with faith-ful work-ers banding,

f In His vine-yard Christ doth need you, This is the day !
Feel the joy there's no re-veal-ing, This is the day !
Strive to reach the heav'n-ly land-ing, This is the day !

THE GOSPEL FEAST—Concluded.

Hear the blessed in-vi-ta-tion, Come to the feast!
Come, come, come to the feast, the Gos-pel feast!

GRACE DIVINE AND FREE.

WM. EDW. PENNEY.
Copyright, 1896, by Asa Hull.
ASA HULL.

1. High-er than the mountain top, Deeper than the sea, Is the measure
2. Wid-er than the u-ni-verse, Stronger than the grave, Is the grace di-
3. Sweetest of the songs that sound O'er the crystal sea, Ring-eth out the
4. When I stand be-fore the throne, And my Saviour see, This will be my

CHORUS.

of the grace That saves me. Grace saves you, and grace saves me, Grace di-
vine that doth My soul save.
glad re-frain, "Grace saved me!"
song a-lone, "Grace saved me!"

vine and free! Hal-le-lu-jah! hal-le-lu-jah! Hal-le-lujah, grace saves me!

WHOLLY THE LORD'S.

Miss P. J. OWENS. W. J. KIRKPATRICK.

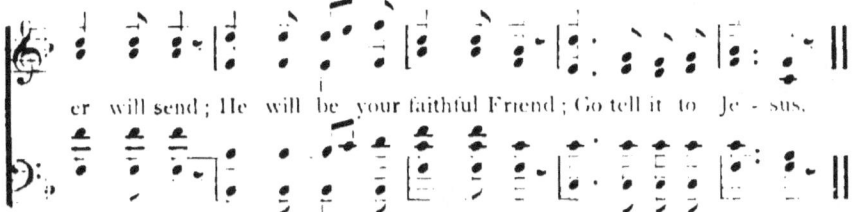

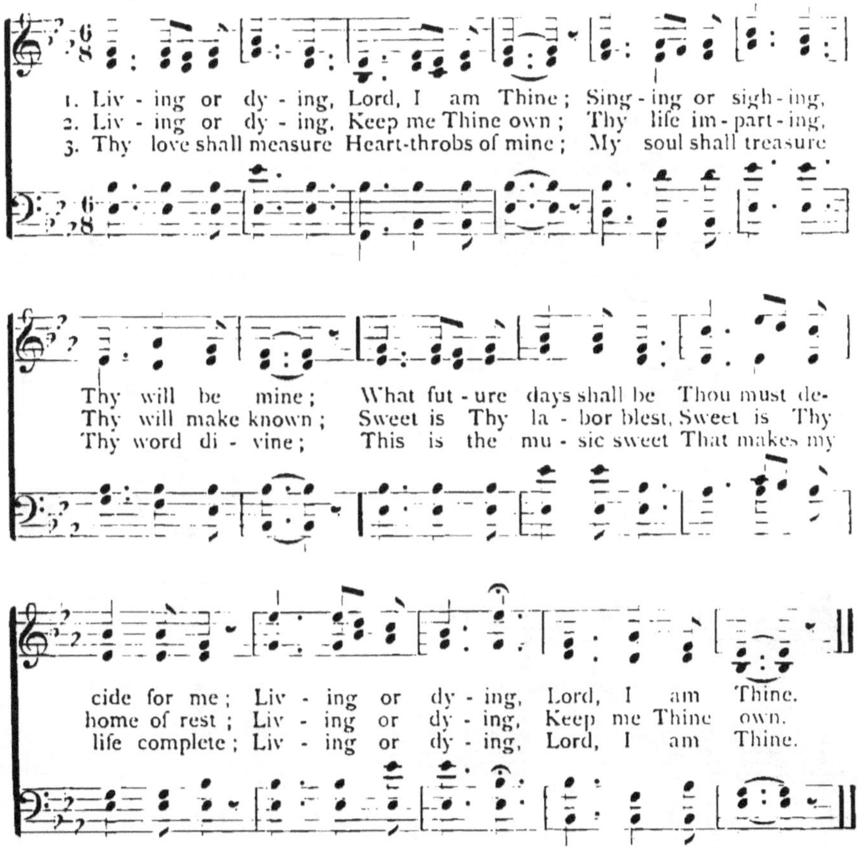

LABOR FOR THE MASTER — Concluded.

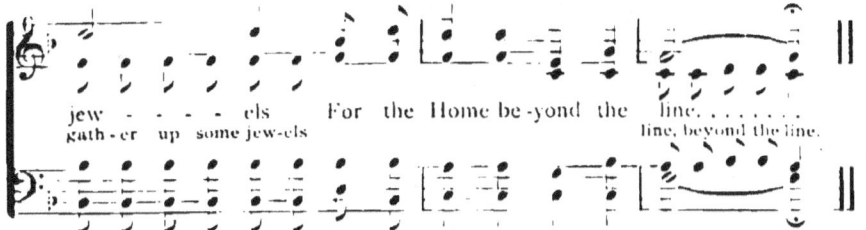

jew - - - els For the Home be-yond the line.........
gath-er up some jew-els   line, beyond the line.

SO WILL I COMFORT THEE.

MARY D. JAMES.   Copyright, 1880, by Asa Hull.   W. J. KIRKPATRICK.

1. So will I com-fort thee, Poor sorrowing child of care; Thy heav-y
2. So will I com-fort thee, Thro' all life's drear-y way; I'll be thy

load of woe Up-on my heart I bear. I know thy pains, and griefs, and fears,
constant guide, I'll keep thee night and day; No foes, no per-ils need'st thou fear,

I hear thy sighs, and count thy tears: So will I com-fort, com-fort thee.
For I, thy God, am al-ways near: So will I com-fort, com-fort thee.

3 So will I comfort thee,
   E'en I, the *mighty God;*
    Unchanging is My love,
    Unfailing is My word.
  No mother's love can equal Mine,
  No arms so strong as arms Divine;
    So will I comfort thee.

4 So will I comfort thee;
    From every stormy blast,
    I'll hide thee with My wings,
    Till all life's storms are past,
  Then bear thee to the heavenly shore,
  Where sorrow's tears shall fall no more:
    So will I comfort thee.

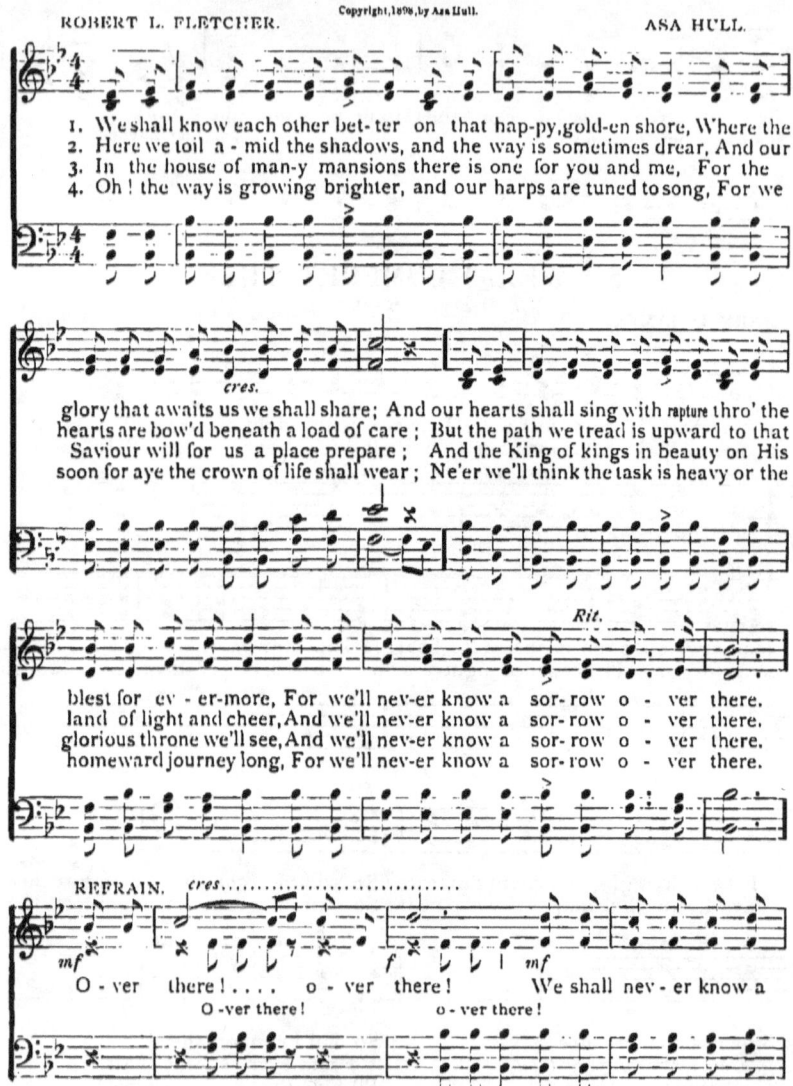

THE HAPPY, GOLDEN SHORE—Concluded.

COME!

MARY D. JAMES.   Copyright, 1898, by Asa Hull.   REV. R. W. TODD.

1. Come, wea-ry wand'rer to thy rest; Come to thy loving Saviour's breast; Come
2. Come with thy fear, and guilt, and sin; For Je-sus takes poor sinners in; He
3. When my sad, weary spirit heard, That precious "come," that blessed word; Down
4. And I did come; O, yes; I've come, And found in Jesus my blest home: No

now to Jesus and be blest; Come, weary wand'rer, come, Come, weary wand'rer come!
died himself, thy soul to win; Come, guilty sinner, come, Come, guilty sinner come.
to my spirit's depth's it stir'd; I said, "I'll come, I'll come!" I said, "I'll come, I'll come!"
more from His dear side to roam: O, I'm so glad I've come! O, I'm so glad I've come!

THE RACE IS ON.—Concluded.

ev - 'ry bur - den down, So run the race that thou ob-tain the crown.

4 "The race is on," while angels from above,
Are watching thee, and beck'ning thee in love,
With the redeemed, who once endured the strife,
Have reached the goal, and entered into life.

5 "The race is on." Lo! this is not thy rest,
That lies beyond, among the pure and blest;
The sunlit towers, all radiant with light,
In grandeur rise on the enraptured sight.

ROCK OF AGES.

A. M. TOPLADY. DR. T. HASTINGS.

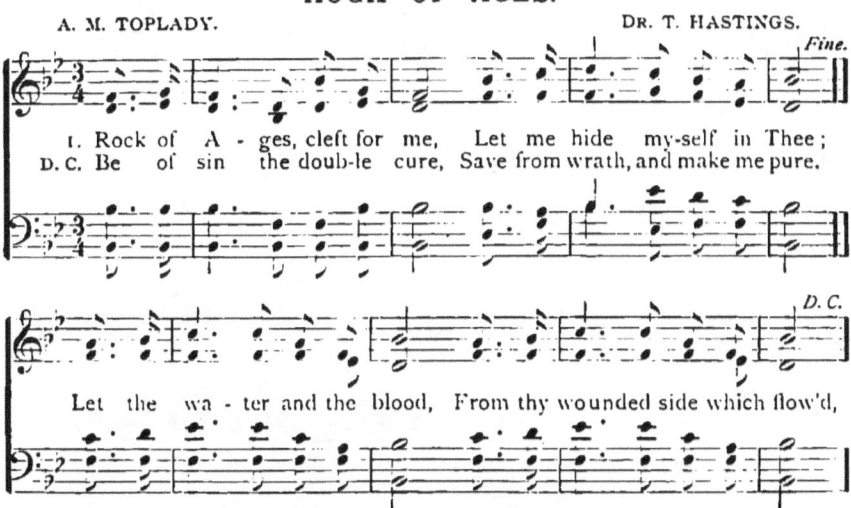

1. Rock of A - ges, cleft for me, Let me hide my-self in Thee;
D.C. Be of sin the doub-le cure, Save from wrath, and make me pure.

Let the wa - ter and the blood, From thy wounded side which flow'd,

2 Could my tears for ever flow,
Could my zeal no languor know,
These for sin could not atone:
Thou must save, and Thou alone:
In my hand no price I bring;
Simply to Thy cross I cling.

3 While I draw this fleeting breath,
When my eyes shall close in death,
When I rise to worlds unknown,
And behold Thee on Thy throne,—
Rock of Ages, cleft for me,
Let me hide myself in Thee.

CROWN HIM LORD OF ALL—Concluded.

Bring forth the royal diadem, And crown Him Lord of all!

4 Let every kindred, every tribe,
   On this terrestrial ball,
  To Him all majesty ascribe,
   And crown Him Lord of all!

5 Oh, that with yonder sacred throng,
   We at His feet may fall!
  We'll join the everlasting song,
   And crown Him Lord of all!

HARWELL.

THOS. KELLY. LOWEL MASON.

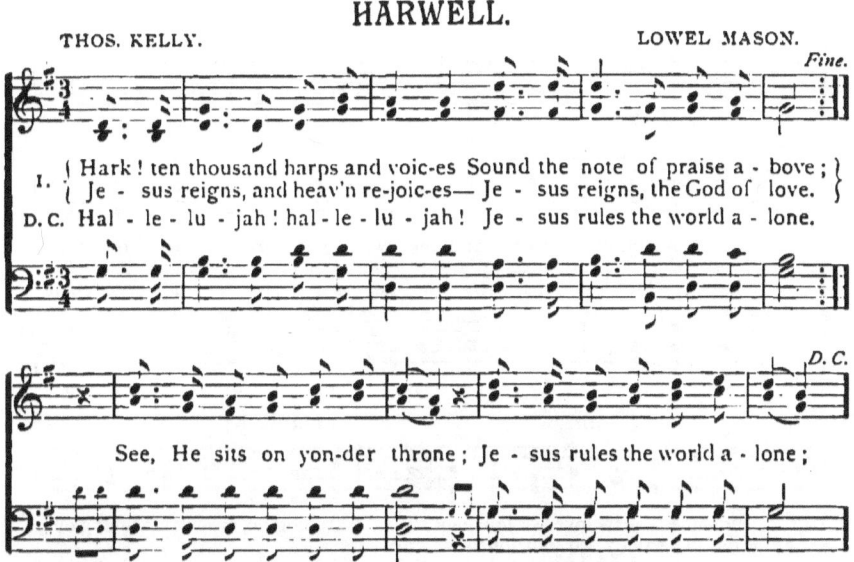

1. Hark! ten thousand harps and voic-es Sound the note of praise a-bove;
   Je-sus reigns, and heav'n re-joic-es— Je-sus reigns, the God of love.
D.C. Hal-le-lu-jah! hal-le-lu-jah! Je-sus rules the world a-lone.

See, He sits on yon-der throne; Je-sus rules the world a-lone;

2 King of glory, reign forever—
   Thine an everlasting crown;
  Nothing from Thy love shall sever
   Those whom Thou hast made Thine own;
  Happy objects of Thy grace, [own;
  Destined to behold Thy face;
   Hallelujah! hallelujah!
  Destined to behold Thy face.

3 Saviour, hasten Thine appearing;
   Bring, O bring the glorious day,
  When the awful summons hearing,
   Heav'n and earth shall pass away.
  Then, with golden harps, we'll sing,
   "Glory, glory to our King!"
   Hallelujah! hallelujah!
  Glory, glory to our King!

WE ARE MARCHING ON—Concluded.

Marching on in the good old way; We're seeking a land more bright, Where cometh no shades of night, We are marching, marching on!

SOFTLY NOW THE LIGHT OF DAY.

G. W. DOANE.   GEORGE HEWS.

1. Soft-ly now the light of day Fades up-on my sight a-way;
2. Soon, for me, the light of day Shall for-ev-er pass a-way;

Free from care, from la-bor free, Lord, I would commune with Thee.
Then, from sin and sor-row free, Take me, Lord, to dwell with Thee.

3 Thou, whose all-pervading eye,
   Naught escapes without, within,
  Pardon each infirmity,
   Open fault, and secret sin.

4 Thou who, sinless, yet hast known
   All of man's infirmity;
  Then from Thine eternal throne,
   Jesus, look with pitying eye.

THE HAVEN OF PEACE—Concluded.

THE BREAD OF LIFE.

M. A. LATHBURY. WM. F. SHERWIN.

1. Break Thou the bread of life, Dear Lord, to me, As Thou didst break the loaves Beside the sea;
2. Bless Thou the truth, dear Lord, To me, to me, As Thou didst bless the bread By Galilee;

Beyond the sacred page I seek Thee, Lord; My spirit pants for Thee, O living Word!
Then shall all bondage cease, All fetters fall; And I shall find my peace, My all-in-all!

ALWAYS TRUE—Concluded.

2 Come, Thou Incarnate Word,
   Gird on Thy mighty sword,
   Our prayer attend;
   Come and Thy people bless,
   And give Thy word success;
   Spirit of holiness,
     On us descend.

3 Come, Holy Comforter,
   Thy sacred witness bear,
   In this glad hour;
   Thou who almighty art,
   Now rule in every heart,
   And ne'er from us depart,
     Spirit of power.

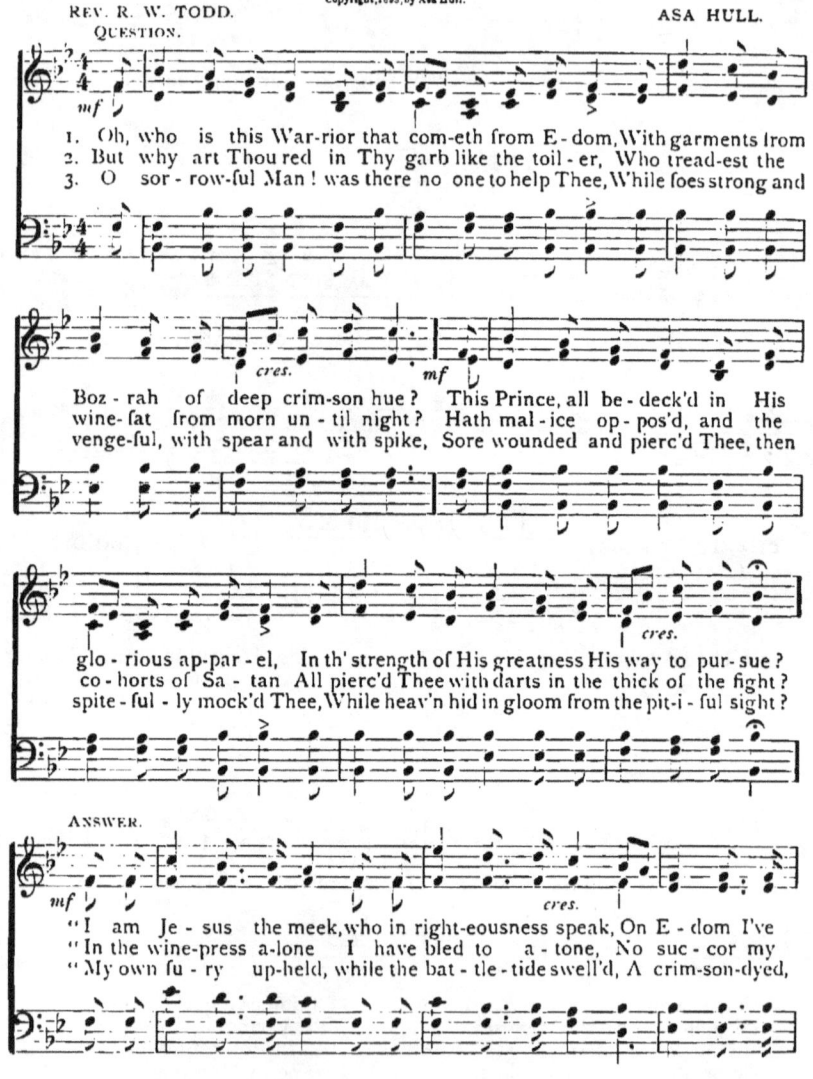

THE MIGHTY TO SAVE—Concluded.

4.

QUESTION. O Warrior and King! tell me what is Thy mission,
  With garments so gory, and armor of might?
  Why comest Thou thus? Wilt Thou smite and destroy me,
  And banish me hence to the shadows of night?
ANSWER. "O'er the battle-field's length, in my greatness and strength,
  I've traveled through death and the grave:
  But the fight was for thee, 'tis thy glad jubilee;
  I am Jesus, the Mighty to Save!"
REFRAIN. The Mighty to Save! yes, mighty to save!
  Hallelujah to Jesus, THE MIGHTY TO SAVE!

BE UP AND DOING—Concluded.

STAND UP! STAND UP FOR JESUS!

G. DUFFIELD.   TUNE—WEBB.

1 STAND up! stand up for Jesus!
   Ye soldiers of the cross;
   Lift high His royal banner,
   It must not suffer loss;
   From victory unto victory
   His army He shall lead,
   Till every foe is vanquished,
   And Christ is Lord indeed.

2 Stand up! stand up for Jesus!
   Stand in His strength alone;
   The arm of flesh will fail you—
   Ye dare not trust your own;
   Put on the Gospel armor,
   And, watching unto prayer,
   Where duty calls, or danger,
   Be never wanting there.

3 Stand up! stand up for Jesus!
   The strife will not be long;
   This day the noise of battle,
   The next the victor's song;
   To him that overcometh,
   A crown of life shall be;
   He with the King of Glory
   Shall reign eternally.

LIGHT—Concluded.

mf Let there be light!... Let there be light!... *mf* Let there be light!... *ff*

"Twas Might Divine roll'd back the screen, And said, "Let there be light!"
They hymn'd the word the Father spoke, Who said, "Let there be light!"
Then from the realms of love the sound Broke forth, "Let there be light!"
Oh, let the anthem swell till all Shall see Redemption's light!

JESUS, SAVIOUR, PILOT ME.

EDW. HOPPER.   J. E. GOULD.

1. Jesus, Saviour, pilot me Over life's tempestuous sea;
D.C. Chart and compass came from Thee: Jesus, Saviour, pilot me.
Unknown waves before me roll, Hiding rock and treach'rous shoal;

2 As a mother stills her child,
Thou canst hush the ocean wild;
Boist'rous waves obey Thy will,
When Thou say'st to them "Be still!"
Wondrous Sovereign of the sea,
Jesus, Saviour, pilot me.

3 When at last I near the shore,
And the fearful breakers roar,
'Twixt me and the peaceful rest,
Then, while leaning on Thy breast,
May I hear Thee say to me,
"Fear not, I will pilot thee!"

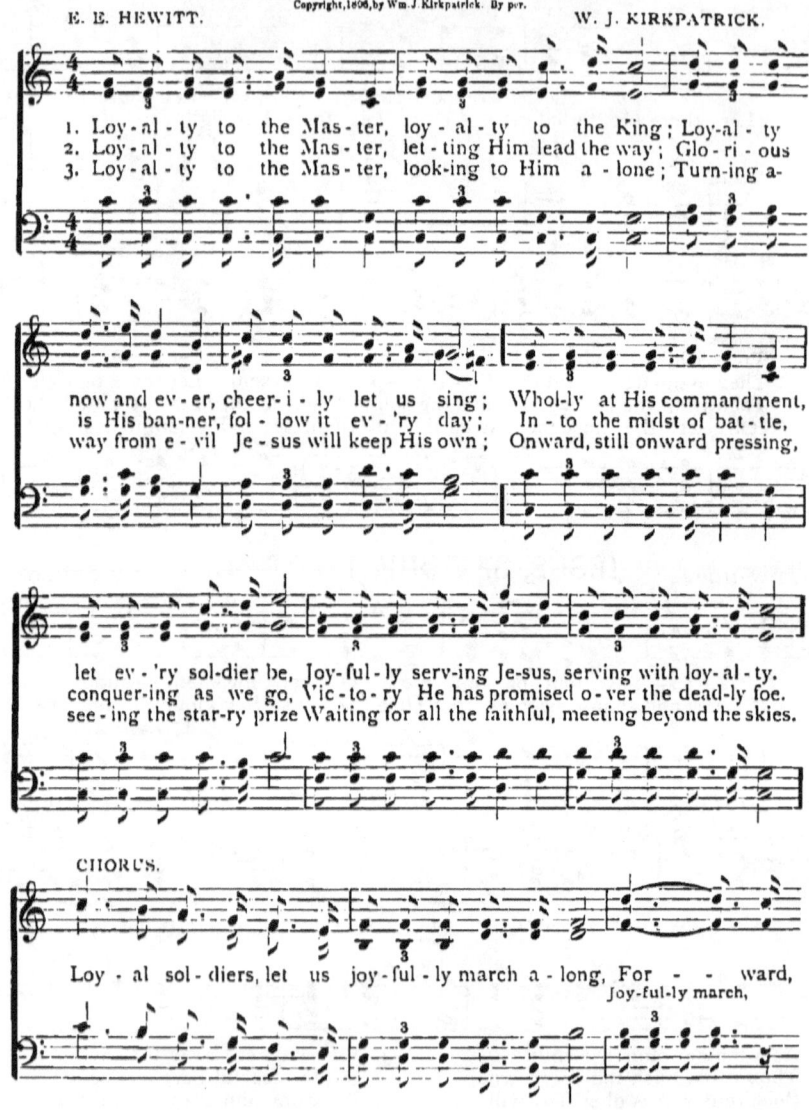

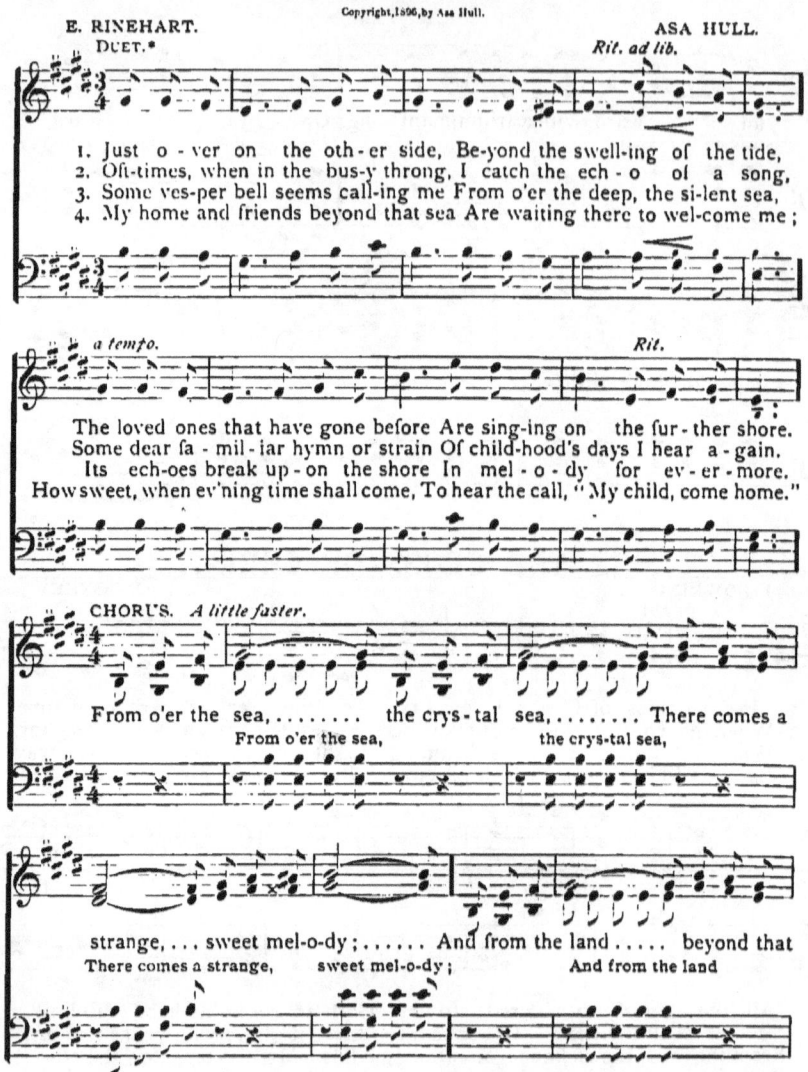

FROM O'ER THE SEA.—Concluded. 69

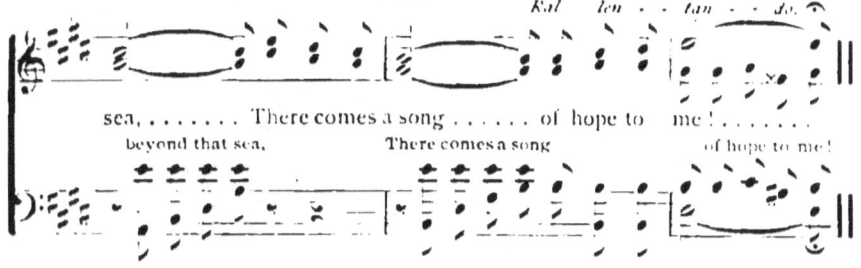

sea,...... There comes a song...... of hope to me!......
beyond that sea,   There comes a song   of hope to me!

FORGET ME NOT.

Copyright,1894,by Asa Hull.

WM. EDW. PENNEY.   ASA HULL.

1. "For-get me not,"........ we oft-en say,...... When friend from
   "For-get me not,"   we oft-en say,

friend..... is torn a-way;..... Forget me not...... when ocean
When friend from friend   is torn a-way;   Forget me not

wide....... Between us rolls...... its might-y tide........
when ocean wide   Between us rolls its might-y tide, its mighty tide.

2 "Forget me not," our sad hearts cry,
While weary years of waiting fly ;
Forget me not, we sigh at last,
When life's short day for us is past.

3 "Forget me not," the Christian cries,
His face upturned toward the skies ;
O Father, whatsoe'er my lot,
In life, in death, forget me not.

TELL THE LOVE OF JESUS—Concluded.

I AM COMING, LORD.

1 I HEAR Thy welcome voice,
   That calls me, Lord, to Thee;
   For cleansing in Thy precious blood,
   That flow'd on Calvary.

CHO. I am coming, Lord!
   Coming now to Thee!
   Wash me, cleanse me, in the blood
   That flow'd on Calvary.

2 Though coming weak and vile,
   Thou dost my strength assure;
   Thou dost my vileness fully cleanse,
   Till spotless all, and pure.

3 'Tis Jesus calls me on
   To perfect faith and love,
   To perfect hope, and peace, and trust,
   For earth and heav'n above.

4 And He the witness gives
   To loyal hearts and free,
   That every promise is fulfilled,
   If faith but brings the plea.

5 All hail! atoning blood!
   All hail! redeeming grace!
   All hail! the gift of Christ, our Lord,
   Our Strength and Righteousness.

Rev. L. Hartsough.

PUT ON THE WHOLE ARMOR—Concluded. 73

WORK, FOR THE NIGHT IS COMING.

1 Work, for the night is coming,
  Work through the morning hours,
  Work while the dew is sparkling,
  Work 'mid springing flow'rs;
  Work, when the day grows brighter,
  Work in the glowing sun;
  Work, for the night is coming,
  When man's work is done.

2 Work, for the night is coming,
  Work through the sunny noon;
  Fill brightest hours with labor,—
  Rest comes sure and soon:
  Give ev'ry flying minute
  Something to keep in store;
  Work, for the night is coming,
  When man works no more.

3 Work, for the night is coming,
  Under the sunset skies;
  While their bright tints are glowing,
  Work, for the daylight flies;
  Work, till the last beam fadeth,
  Fadeth to shine no more;
  Work, while the night is dark'ning,
  When man's work is o'er.

4 Work, for the night is coming,
  Work, while the fields are white;
  Work, for thy sands are running,
  Work, while hopes are bright;
  Gather thy sheaves at morning;
  Rest not thy hand at noon;
  Labor and strive till evening;
  Rest when daylight's gone.

THE ARMOR OF GOD—Concluded.

O, THINK OF A HOME OVER THERE.

1. O, THINK of a home over there,
   By the side of the river of light,
   Where the saints, all immortal and fair,
   Are robed in their garments of white.
   ||: Over there, over there, over there,
   O, think of a home over there. :||

2. O, think of the friends over there,
   Who before us the journey have trod,
   Of the songs that they breathe on the air,
   In their home in the palace of God.
   ||: Over there, over there, over there,
   O, think of the friends over there. :||

3. My Saviour is now over there;   [rest:
   There my kindred and friends are at
   Then away from my sorrow and care,
   Let me fly to the land of the blest.
   ||: Over there, over there, over there,
   My Saviour is now over there. :||

4. I'll soon be at home over there,
   For the end of my journey I see;
   Many dear to my heart, over there,
   Are watching and waiting for me.
   ||: Over there, over there, over there,
   I'll soon be at home over there. :||

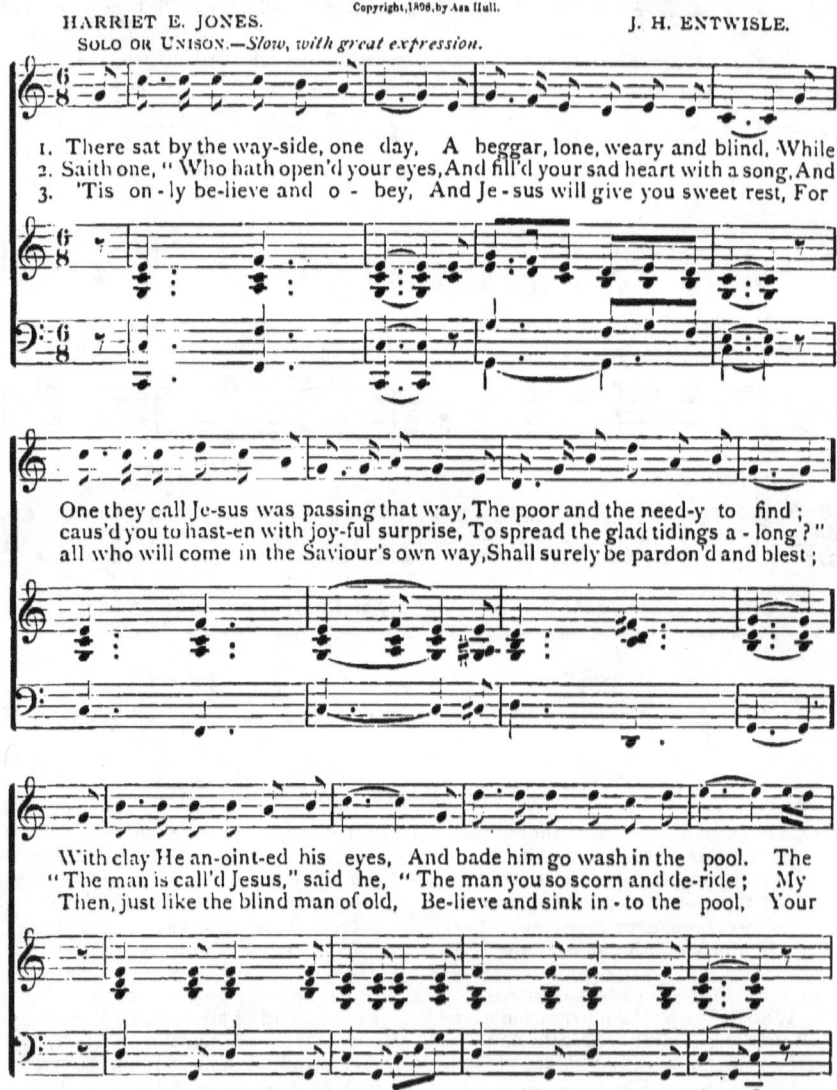

AT THE POOL OF SILOAM—Concluded.

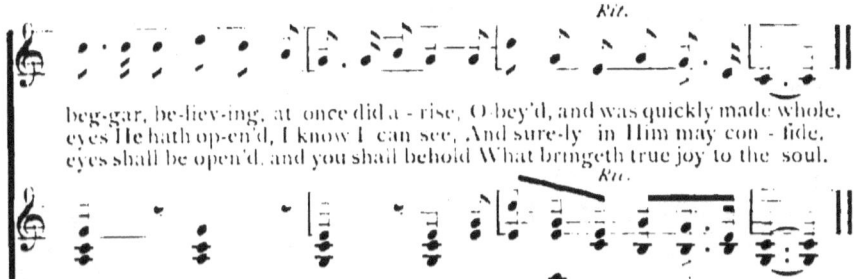

beg-gar, be-liev-ing, at once did a-rise, Obey'd, and was quickly made whole.
eyes He hath op-en'd, I know I can see, And sure-ly in Him may con - fide.
eyes shall be open'd, and you shall behold What bringeth true joy to the soul.

NOTE.— *One or more stanzas of* "THE CLEANSING FOUNTAIN" *may be sung with fine effect by the whole Congregation at the conclusion of the foregoing.*

THE CLEANSING FOUNTAIN.

COWPER.

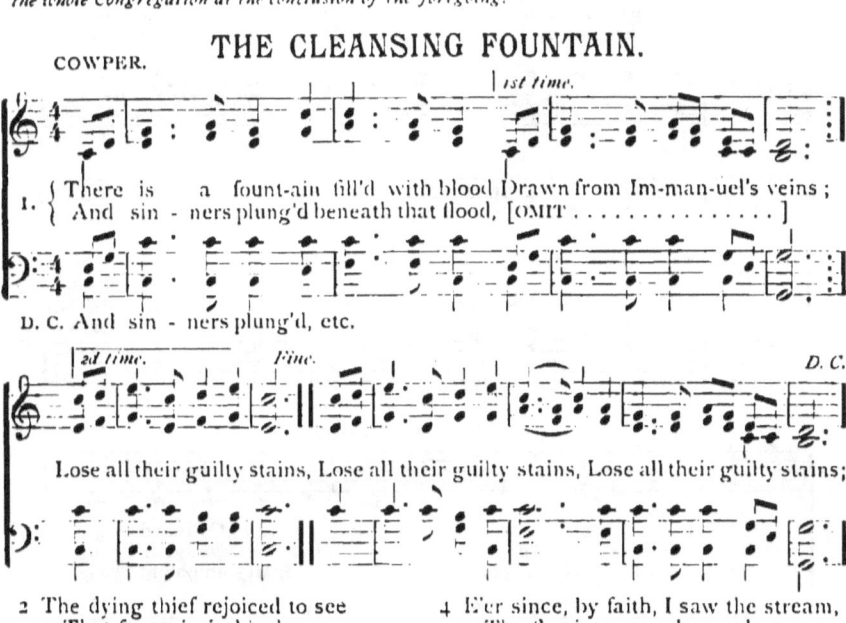

1. There is a fount-ain fill'd with blood Drawn from Im-man-uel's veins;
And sin - ners plung'd beneath that flood, [OMIT ....]
D. C. And sin - ners plung'd, etc.

Lose all their guilty stains, Lose all their guilty stains, Lose all their guilty stains;

2 The dying thief rejoiced to see
  That fountain in his day;
And there may I, though vile as he,
  Wash all my sins away.

3 Dear dying Lamb! Thy precious blood
  Shall never lose its power,
Till all the ransomed Church of God,
  Are saved, to sin no more.

4 E'er since, by faith, I saw the stream,
  Thy flowing wounds supply,
Redeeming love has been my theme,
  And shall be till I die.

5 Then in a nobler, sweeter song,
  I'll sing Thy power to save,
When this poor, lisping, stamm'ring
  Lies silent in the grave. [tongue,

THE CHRISTIAN SOLDIER.—Concluded.

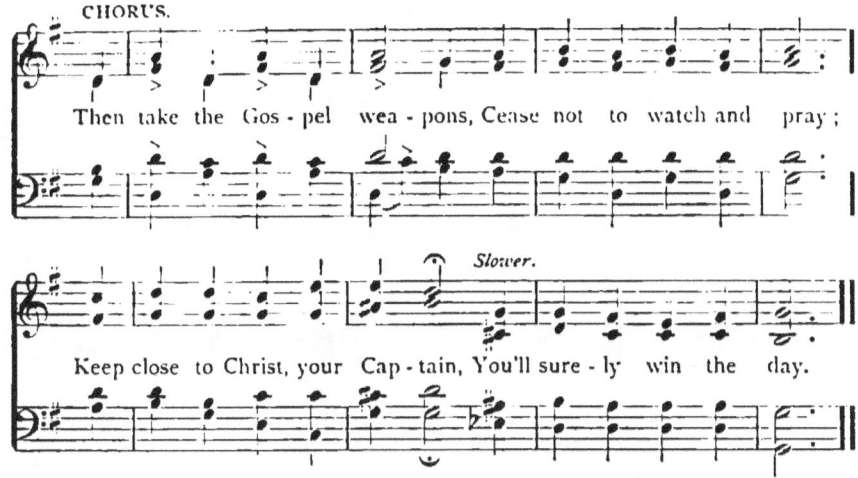

Then take the Gospel weapons, Cease not to watch and pray;
Keep close to Christ, your Captain, You'll surely win the day.

GOD'S WONDROUS LOVE.

MRS. L. M. B. BATEMAN.   ASA HULL.

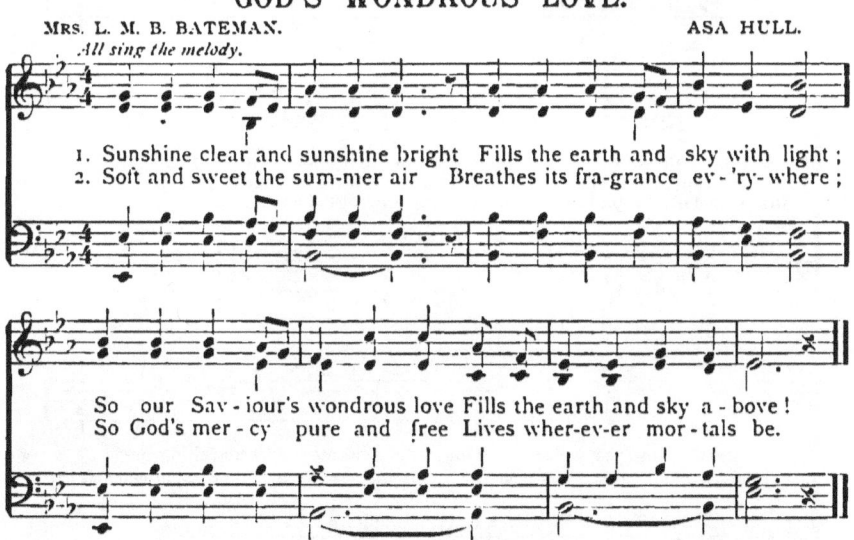

1. Sunshine clear and sunshine bright Fills the earth and sky with light;
2. Soft and sweet the summer air Breathes its fragrance ev-'ry-where;

So our Saviour's wondrous love Fills the earth and sky above!
So God's mercy pure and free Lives wher-ev-er mor-tals be.

3 Raindrops fall and falls the dew,
  Ever bounteous, ever new;
  As the river seeks the sea
  God's great kindness floweth free!

4 Notes of gladness, words of praise,
  Let our hearts and voices raise;
  May our love and service be
  His through all eternity.

IN SWEET BY-AND-BY.

I. N. McHOSE. I. N. McHOSE.

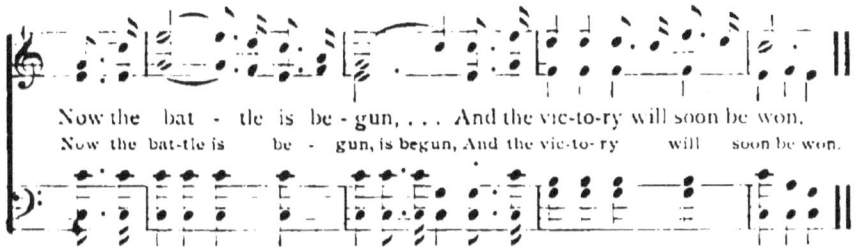

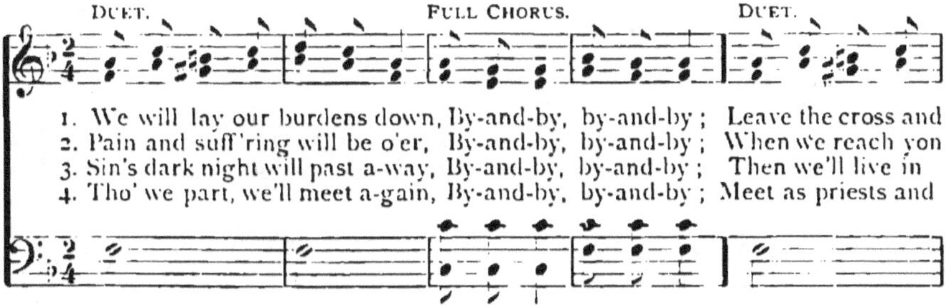

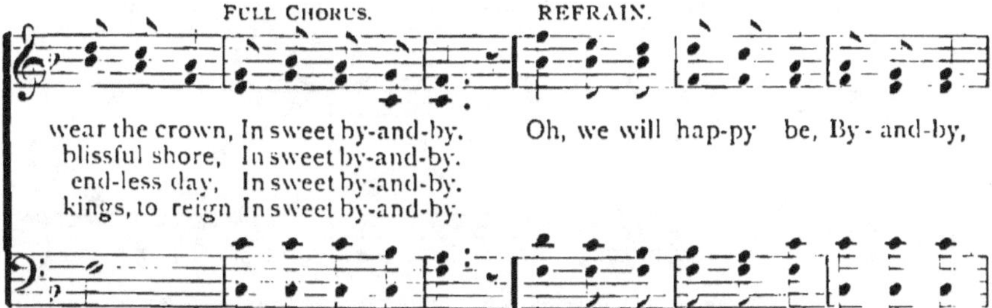

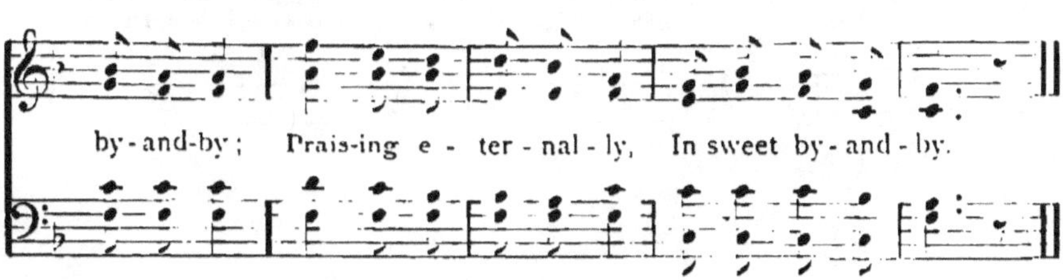

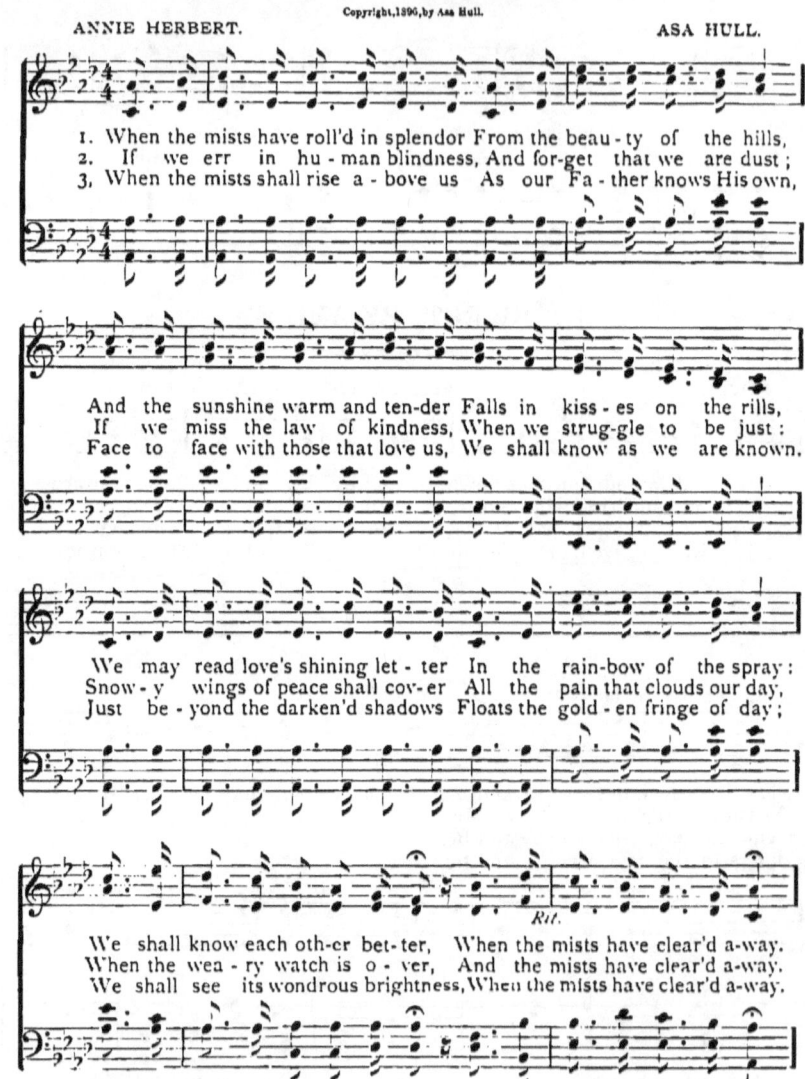

BEYOND THE SHADOWS.—Concluded.

JESUS, REFUGE OF MY SOUL.

C. WESLEY.   *Music on page 227.*

1 JESUS, refuge of my soul,
   Let me to Thy bosom fly,
While the nearer waters roll,
   While the tempest still is high ;
Hide me, O my Saviour, hide,
   Till the storm of life is past ;
Safe into the haven guide,
   O receive my soul at last.

2 Other refuge have I none ;
   Hangs my helpless soul on Thee :
Leave, O leave me not alone ;
   Still support and comfort me :
All my trust on Thee is stay'd ;
   All my help from Thee I bring ;
Cover my defenceless head
   With the shadow of Thy wing.

3 Thou, O Christ, art all I want :
   More than all in Thee I find :
Raise the fallen, cheer the faint,
   Heal the sick, and lead the blind,
Just and holy is Thy name ;
   I am all unrighteousness ;
False, and full of sin I am ;
   Thou art full of truth and grace.

4 Plenteous grace with Thee is found,
   Grace to cover all my sin :
Let the healing streams abound ;
   Make and keep me pure within.
Thou of life the fountain art ;
   Freely let me take of Thee :
Spring Thou up within my heart ;
   Rise to all eternity.

JESUS IS COMING AGAIN—Concluded.

GLORIOUS EASTER DAY.

HARRY SANDERS.   Copyright, 1891, by Asa Hull.   HARRY SANDERS.

Allegro.

1. This is glo-rious East-er day, Glory hal-le-lu-jah! Come and sing an East-er lay, Glo-ry hal-le-lu-jah! Lives a-gain our might-y King, Glo-ry hal-le-lu-jah! Death has lost its venom'd sting, Glory hal-le-lu-jah!
2. Look in-to the va-cant tomb, Glory hal-le-lu-jah! Van-ish'd all its fear-ful gloom, Glo-ry hal-le-lu-jah! See! the stone is roll'd a-way, Glo-ry hal-le-lu-jah! Je-sus lives! O joyous day! Glory hal-le-lu-jah!
3. Now in might-y pow'r He reigns, Glory hal-le-lu-jah! End-ed all His griefs and pains, Glo-ry hal-le-lu-jah! He hath all our ran-soms paid, Glo-ry hal-le-lu-jah! Full atonement He hath made, Glory hal-le-lu-jah!

THE CLEANSING STREAM—Concluded. 91

flow,...... And all my sins...... are white as snow......
the precious flow, And all my sins are white as snow.

2 No other hope but this will stand,
All other ground is shifting sand;
One only sure foundation 's giv'n,
On which to build a hope of heav'n.

3 No righteousness I'll trust of mine,
But build upon a hope divine;

And I will sing while ages roll,
The blood of Christ hath made me whole.

4 By faith the blood is now applied,
That flowed from my Redeemer's side;
And in that flow, that precious flow,
My sins are washed as white as snow.

ISAAC WATTS.   **CHRISTMAS.**   HANDEL.

1. Come, let us lift our joy-ful eyes Up to the courts a-bove,
2. Come, let us bow be-fore His feet, And venture near the Lord;

And smile to see our Fa-ther there, Up-on a throne of love,
No fi-'ry cher-ub guards His seat, Nor doub-le-flaming sword,

Up-on a throne of love.
Nor double-flam-ing sword.

3 The peaceful gates of heavenly bliss,
Are opened by the Son;
High let us raise our notes of praise,
And reach th' almighty throne.

4 To Thee ten thousand thanks we bring,
Great Advocate on high;
And glory to th' eternal King,
Who lays His anger by.

THE FATHER'S PROMISES—Concluded.

4 Oh, precious words of promise!
  They shall never know decay,
For nothing dims their brightness,
  They are just the same for aye;
Each promise is a jewel
  With a lustre rich and rare,
No glitt'ring gem of monarch
  With such beauty can compare.

THE SABBATH SCHOOL.—Concluded.

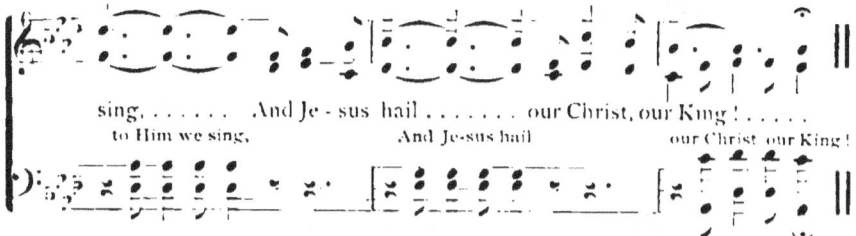

THE BORDER LINE.

E. R. LATTA. CHAS. EDW. POLLOCK.
Copyright, 1896, by Asa Hull.

1. Oh, the beauties we shall see, When we reach the land divine!
   We shall know the mystery When we cross the border line.
2. There, 'tis day, without the sun, For the face of God doth shine;
   And the night shall ne'er come on, When we cross the border line.

D.S. With a gladness of the heart Shall we cross the border line?

CHORUS.
When we're bidden to depart, Shall we know the countersign?

3 There, we shall no burden bear,
  And our hearts shall ne'er repine ;
  We shall never know a care,
  When we cross the border line.

4 Help us Lord, to pray the prayer,
  "Not my will be done, but Thine !"
  We will praise Thee, over there,
  When we cross the border line.

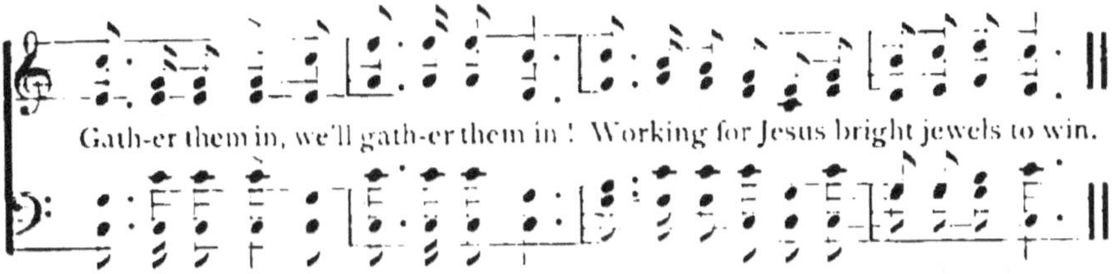

WORKING FOR JESUS—Concluded.

Gath-er them in, we'll gath-er them in! Working for Jesus bright jewels to win.

YOUTHFUL PRAISE.

ARR. BY HARRY SANDERS.   Copyright,1870,by Asa Hull.

1. { Je - sus! in Thy glo-rious dwelling, Where the heav'nly an - thems ring,
   { Dost Thou hear the children sing-ing, [OMIT . . . .]
2. { Je - sus! from the glo - ry round Thee Dost Thou look with smiling face,
   { When the children's hands are lift - ed, [OMIT . . . .]

CHORUS.

Dost Thou heed the praise they bring? Glory, glory, halle-lu-jah! From the riv-er
Low-ly pray-ing for Thy grace?

to the sea; Sweet the voices of the children, Singing praises un-to Thee.

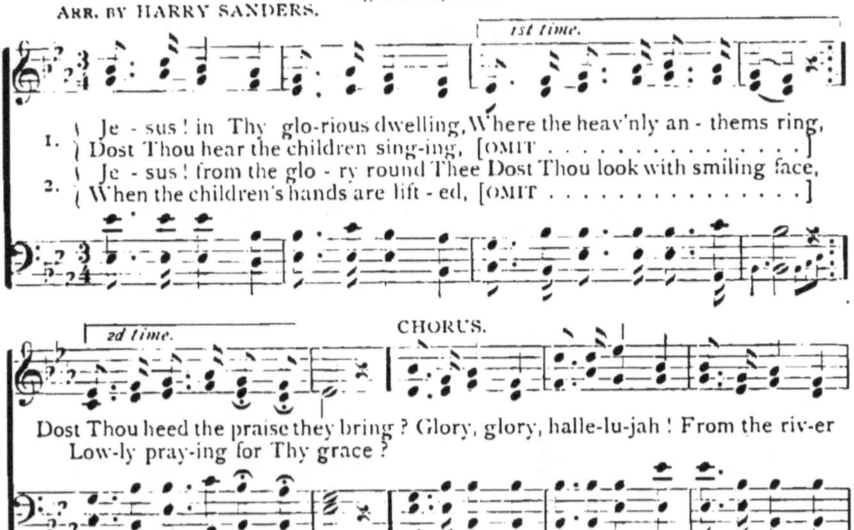

3 Jesus! though we cannot see Thee,
  Art Thou still our watchful guide?
  Doth Thy loving whisper call us?
  Doth Thy tender hand provide?

4 Jesus! Thou wilt never leave us,
  Till our feet at last shall stand,
  With the choir of angels singing,
  Evermore at Thy right hand.

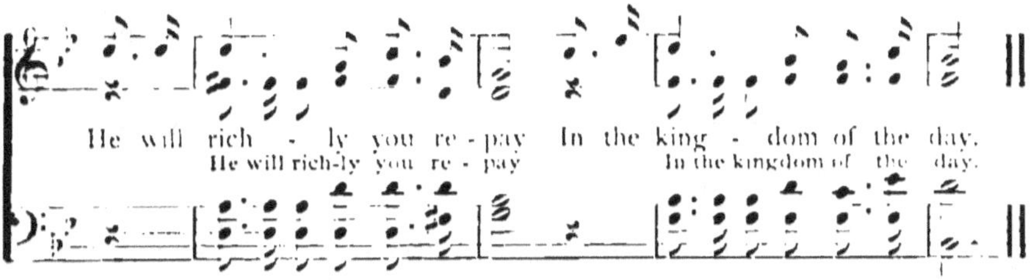

SOW AND GATHER—Concluded.

He will rich - ly you re - pay In the king - dom of the day.
He will rich-ly you re - pay In the kingdom of the day.

ONWARD, RIGHT ONWARD.

P. S. HOWELL.   ASA HULL.

1. Onward, right onward! Heeding no toil or pain; Onward, right onward!
2. Onward, tho' round us Billows may roll and toss; Onward, tho' hearts ache,
3. Onward and upward! Nev-er so dark a time, But beams from heaven

Ea - ger the prize to gain. Darkly the clouds may gather, Cold-ly the
Moaning with sense of loss. Close-ly be-side us walk-eth Death with his
In - to our pathway shine. Nev-er in deep-est sor-row O - ver our

Rit.

rain may fall, Starless the night's deep shadows, But there is light for all.
sa - ble pall; Deep are the pangs he bringeth, Yet there is joy for all.
dead we weep, But that a hope of heav-en In-to our hearts may creep.

THE KING'S BUSINESS, Etc.—Concluded. 105

Ye that are loy-al do not stay, The business of the King hath haste.

BATTLING FOR TEMPERANCE.

R. L. FLETCHER.
Copyright,1898,by Asa Hull.
ASA HULL.

1. The children for temp'rance are gath'ring, With numbers surpassing-ly grand;
2. The arm-or of Christ they are wearing, No mat-ter what others may think;
3. From near and from far they are banding, The young and the fair and the brave;

They're ris-ing with youthful de-vo-tion, And tak-ing a glo-ri-ous stand.
They know that for right they are dar-ing, When battl'ing the curse of strong drink.
For God and for temp'rance they're standing, Our land from intemp'rance to save.

D. S. We'll put on the arm-or, sal-va-tion, And bat-tle for God and the right.

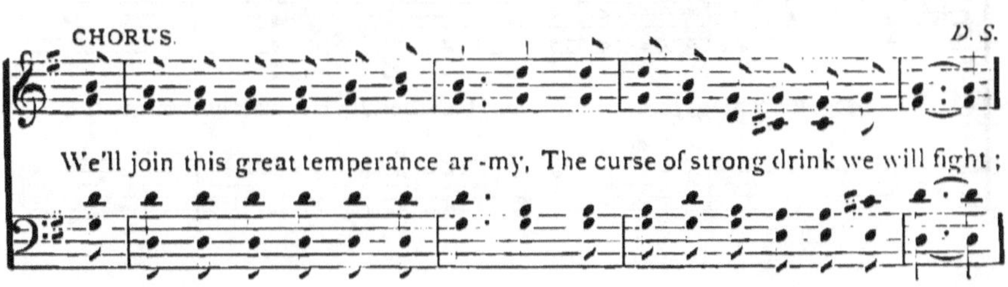

CHORUS.   D. S.

We'll join this great temperance ar-my, The curse of strong drink we will fight;

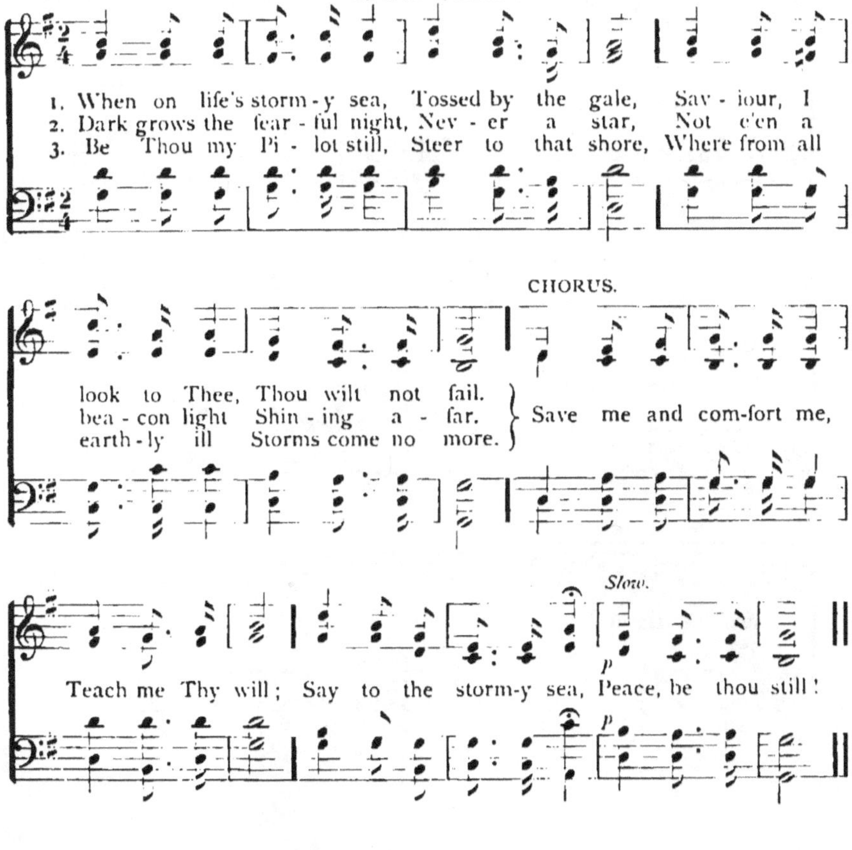

THE CHILDREN'S SONG—Concluded.

Jesus they sang; Ho-san-na, ho-san-na, ho-san-na to Je-sus they sang!
Jesus we'll sing; Ho-san-na, ho-san-na to Je-sus, our Saviour and King!

HIS GUIDING HAND.

E. P. LELAND. Copyright, 1880, by Asa Hull. W. J. KIRKPATRICK.

1. He lead-eth me, He lead-eth me; How sweet to know that Jesus' hand
2. He lead-eth me, He lead-eth me; How calm the weary heart doth grow

Leads me thro' the wilderness In-to the promised Land.
When He leads; and oh, what rest The burden'd soul may know!

CHORUS.
He lead-eth me, He lead-eth me; Like a ten-der shep-herd, He lead-eth me.

3 He leadeth me, He leadeth me;
And knows the paths must thorny be,
Trav'ling up to heav'nly life,
By way of Calvary.

4 He leadeth me, He leadeth me;
It is enough; I'll joyful be,
For I know it is in love
That thus He leadeth me.

BE READY AND OBEY—Concluded.

THE LORD'S PRAYER.

1 Our Father, who art in heaven, hallowed | be thy | name ;
   Thy kingdom come, Thy will be done on | earth, as it | is in | heaven ;

2 Give us this day our | daily | bread ;
   And forgive us our trespasses as we forgive those that | trespass a-| gainst —| us.

3 And lead us not into temptation, but deliver | us from | evil ;
   For Thine is the kingdom, and the power, and the | glory, for | ev-— | er. ‖
   Amen.

THE ARK OF SALVATION.—Concluded.

A song of thanksgiving to Christ on the way, For He is the "Mighty to save!"

LIFE'S FLOWING RIVER.

J. G. PERCIVAL. ARR. BY ASA HULL.

1. Faintly flow, thou fall-ing riv-er, Like a dream that dies a-way;
2. Ros-es bloom, and then they wither, Cheeks are bright, then fade and die;

Down the o-cean glid-ing ev-er, Keep thy calm, un-ruf-fled way;
D. S. To e-ter-ni-ty's dark o-cean, Bury-ing all its treasures there.
Shapes of light are waft-ed hith-er, Then like vis-ions hur-ry by;
D. S. Time is bear-ing us to heav-en, Home of hap-pi-ness and rest.

Time with such a si-lent mo-tion, Floats a-long on wings of air;
Quick as clouds at eve-ning driv-en O'er the man-y col-or'd west,

BEYOND THE GATES.—Concluded.

Chorus: Be-yond the gates,........ O cit-y grand!........
Be-yond the gates, O cit-y grand!
Good cheer a-waits.......... the pil-grim band,.........
Good cheer a-waits the pil-grim band,
Who en-ter at the Lord's command, At the op'ning of the gates!

THE SAVIOUR'S CALL.

T. HASTINGS. ASA HULL.

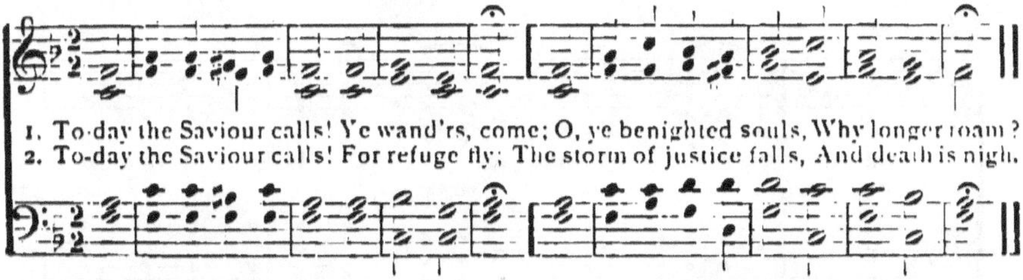

1. To-day the Saviour calls! Ye wand'rs, come; O, ye benighted souls, Why longer roam?
2. To-day the Saviour calls! For refuge fly; The storm of justice falls, And death is nigh.

3 To-day the Saviour calls!
   O, hear Him now:
   Within these sacred walls
     To Jesus bow.

4 The Spirit calls to-day;
   Yield to His power;
   O, grieve Him not away,—
     'Tis mercy's hour.

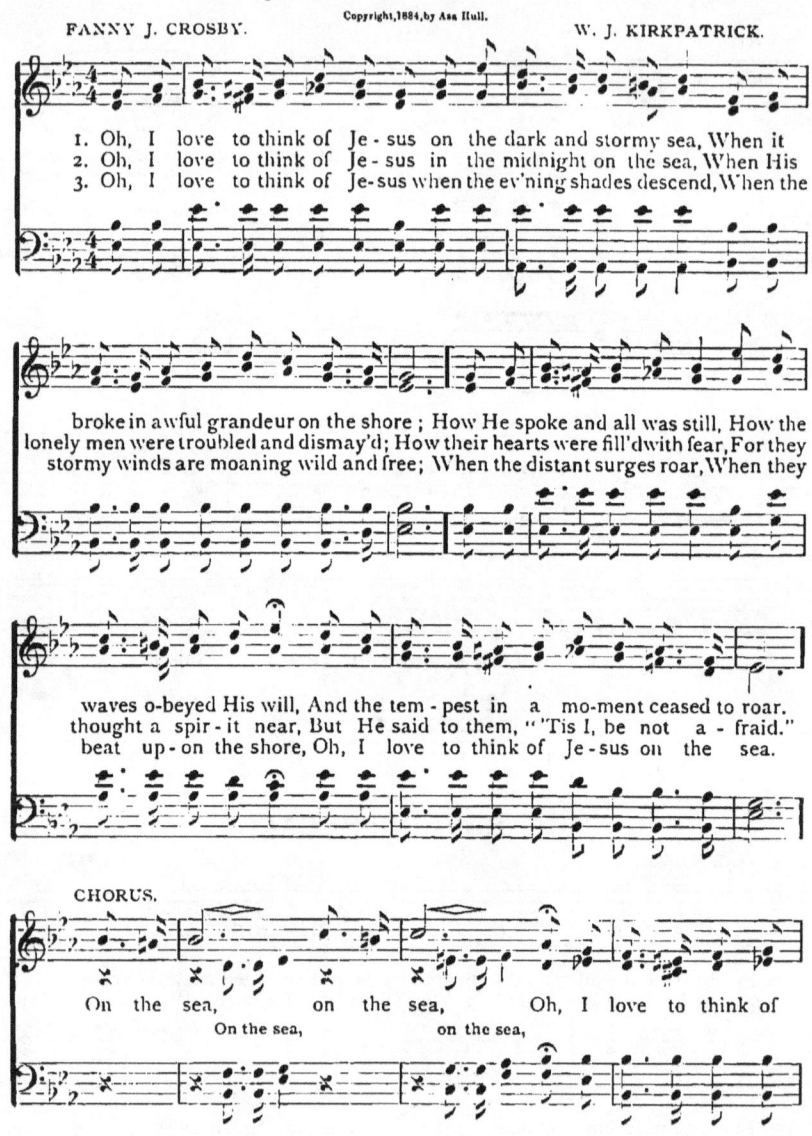

JESUS ON THE SEA—Concluded.

Je-sus on the sea; He whispered, "Peace, be still," And the waves o-bey'd His will; Oh, I love to think of Je-sus on the sea.

MY NAME.

Mrs. E. W. CHAPMAN.   Copyright, 1884, by Asa Hull.   J. H. TENNEY.

1. My name on Je-sus' hands In crim-son lines is traced; And not one let-ter there Can ev-er be ef-fac'd.
2. My name is on His heart, His grace and love are mine; And with His jewels bright, My soul at last shall shine.
3. My name within His book Is writ with pen di-vine; And when with Him I reign, His "New Name" shall be mine.

CHORUS.

My name my Sav-iour knows, He knows from whence I came; And when in heav'n He calls, I'll answer to my name.

IN THE WILDERNESS—Concluded.

THE LORD WILL PROVIDE.

C. S. H. C. S. HARRINGTON.

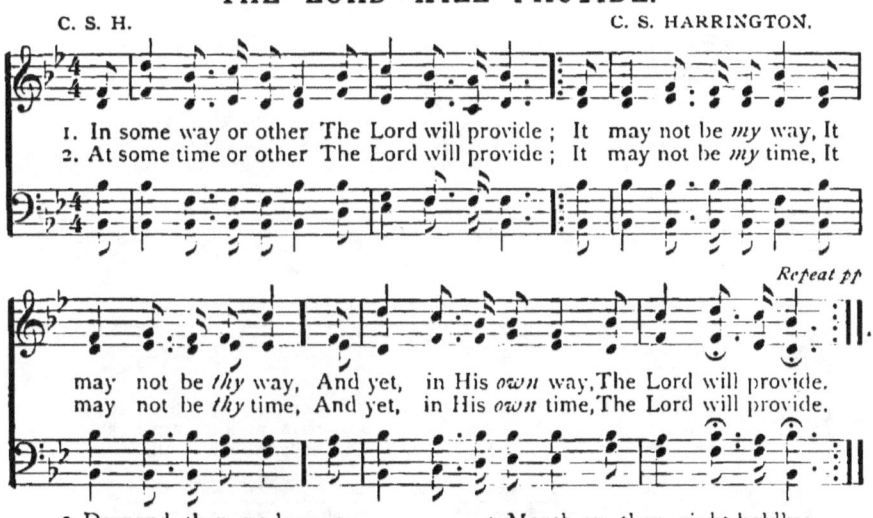

1. In some way or other The Lord will provide; It may not be *my* way, It may not be *thy* way, And yet, in His *own* way, The Lord will provide.

2. At some time or other The Lord will provide; It may not be *my* time, It may not be *thy* time, And yet, in His *own* time, The Lord will provide.

3 Despond, then, no longer;
The Lord will provide;
And this be the token—
No word He hath spoken
Was ever yet broken,—
The Lord will provide.

4 March on, then, right boldly;
The sea shall divide;
The pathway made glorious
With shoutings victorious,
We'll join in the chorus,
The Lord will provide.

AIM HIGH—Concluded.

EVEN ME.

Mrs. E. Codner. Wm. B. Bradbury.

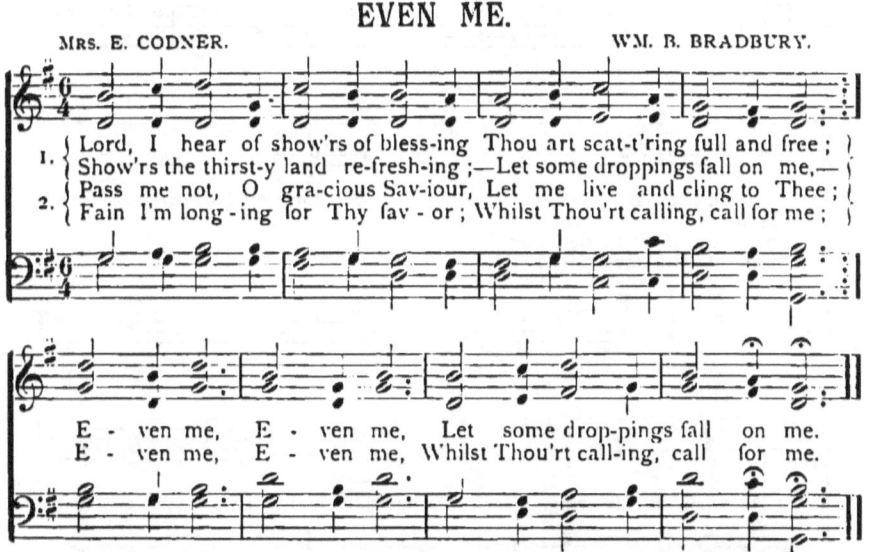

3 Pass me not, O mighty Spirit,
   Thou canst make the blind to see;
  Witnesses of Jesus' merit,
    Speak some word of pow'r to me;
      Even me, even me,
    Speak some word of pow'r to me.

4 Love of God, so pure and changeless,
   Blood of Christ, so rich and free;
  Grace of God, so rich and boundless,
    Magnify it all in me;
      Even me, even me,
    Magnify it all in me.

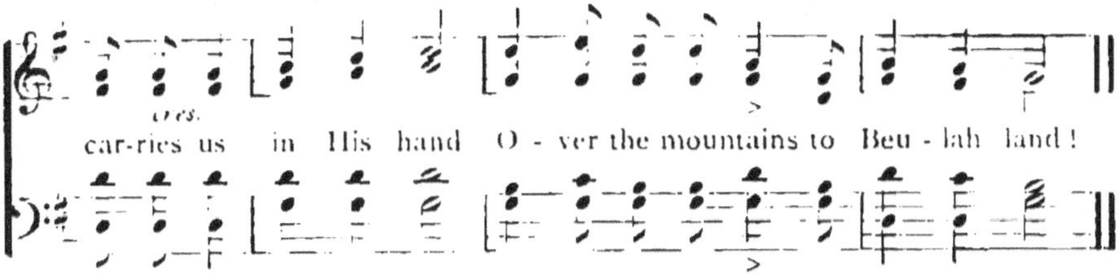

OVER TO BEULAH LAND.—Concluded.

car-ries us in His hand O-ver the mountains to Beu-lah land!

PRAISE THE KING.

ELTA M. LEWIS. Copyright, 1898, by Asa Hull. JNO. R. BRYANT.

1. Praise the ev-er-last-ing King! Let the hills with mu-sic ring;
2. Praise the ev-er-last-ing King! Let the sea its tri-bute bring,
3. Praise the ev-er-last-ing King! Let the flow'rs their censers swing;
4. Praise the ev-er-last-ing King! Sun and moon and stars shall sing;

Let the mountains, tow'ring high, Send the cho-rus to the sky.
And the waves His voice can tame, Swell the tri-bute to His name.
Let the thun-der and the rain, Join the for-est's low re-frain.
Angels 'round His throne proclaim, Praise and glo-ry to His name.

CHORUS. *1st time.* *2nd time.*

{ Praise Him, praise Him, Praises let His people sing;
{ Praise Him, praise Him, [OMIT.............] Praise the ever-last-ing King.

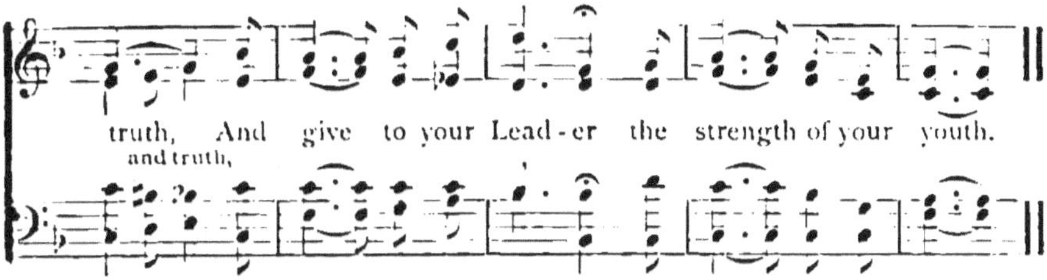

STAND FIRM—Concluded.

truth, And give to your Lead-er the strength of your youth.
and truth,

THE TIME FOR ACTION.

R. S. CUMMINGS. Copyright, 1884, by Asa Hull. S. J. VAIL.

1. If you have a work to do, Wait not till to-morrow; Put-ting off from
2. When you have the golden chance, Help some needy brother; For each blessing
3. What-so-e'er you find to do For yourself or neighbor, Do it now, no

day to day Brings but care and sor-row. Let no short but pre-cious hour
you be-stow God will give an-oth-er. Free-ly give of ev-'ry good
oth-er time Is there giv'n for la-bor,. And when toil and cares are o'er,

Pass you by un-heed-ed, But while time is given you Do the work that's needed.
God to you has giv-en ; And upon you He will shower Choicest gifts from heaven.
Earthly ties shall sever; You shall hear the welcome word, "Come and rest forever."

CROWN HIM FOREVER — Concluded.

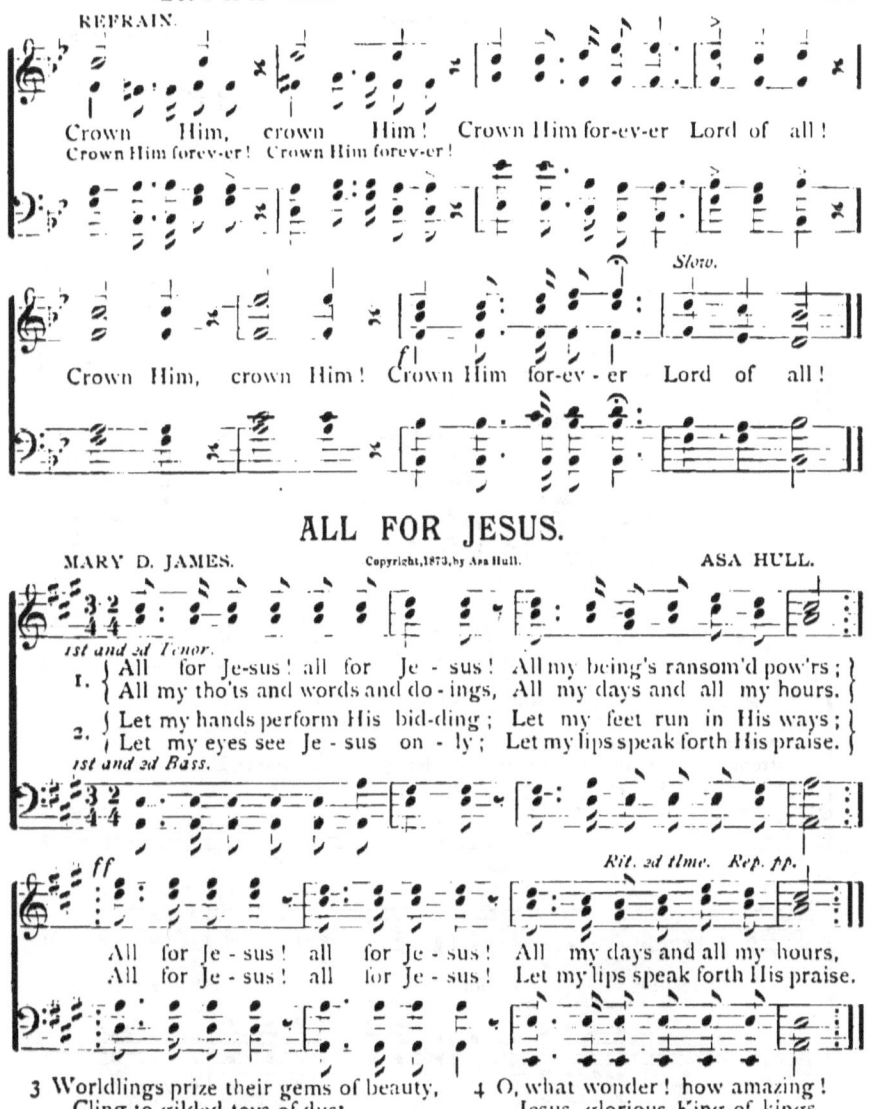

ALL FOR JESUS.

MARY D. JAMES.   Copyright, 1873, by Asa Hull.   ASA HULL.

1. All for Jesus! all for Jesus! All my being's ransom'd pow'rs;
   All my tho'ts and words and doings, All my days and all my hours.

2. Let my hands perform His bidding; Let my feet run in His ways;
   Let my eyes see Jesus only; Let my lips speak forth His praise.

All for Jesus! all for Jesus! All my days and all my hours,
All for Jesus! all for Jesus! Let my lips speak forth His praise.

3 Worldlings prize their gems of beauty,
  Cling to gilded toys of dust,
  Boast of wealth, and fame, and pleasure;
  Only Jesus will I trust,
    Only Jasus! only Jesus!
  Only Jesus will I trust.

4 O, what wonder! how amazing!
  Jesus, glorious King of kings,
  Deigns to call me His beloved,
  Lets me rest beneath His wings.
    All for Jesus! all for Jesus!
  Resting now beneath His wings.

RESTING, SWEETLY RESTING.—Concluded.

ALL FOR JESUS.

MARY D. JAMES. Copyright, 1877, by Asa Hull. ASA HULL.

1. All for Jesus! all for Jesus! All my being's ransom'd pow'rs;
   All my thoughts and words and doings, All my days and all my hours.
2. Let my hands perform His bidding; Let my feet run in His ways;
   Let my eyes see Jesus only; Let my lips speak forth His praise.

All for Jesus! all for Jesus! All my days and all my hours.
All for Jesus! all for Jesus! Let my lips speak forth His praise.

3 Worldlings prize their gems of beauty,
  Cling to gilded toys of dust,
  Boast of wealth, and fame, and pleasure;
  Only Jesus will I trust.
    Only Jesus! only Jesus!
  Only Jesus will I trust.

4 O, what wonder! how amazing!
  Jesus, glorious King of kings,
  Deigns to call me His beloved,
  Lets me rest beneath His wings.
    All for Jesus! all for Jesus!
  Resting now beneath His wings.

JESUS CALLS FOR WORKERS.—Concluded. 133

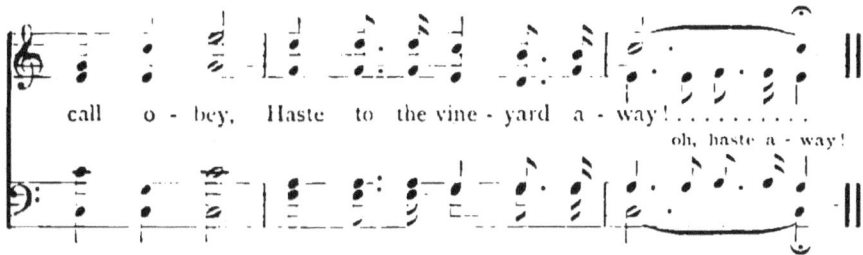

call o-bey, Haste to the vine-yard a-way!.......... oh, haste a-way!

THE HILLS OF AMETHYST.

Copyright,1871,by Asa Hull.

Mrs. P. J. OWENS.   HARRY SANDERS.
Moderato.

1. Lift thine eyes un-to the hills, Thou in sadness weeping; There a joy-ous
2. Dost thou miss the golden grain, Snowy buds immortal? Would'st thou have them

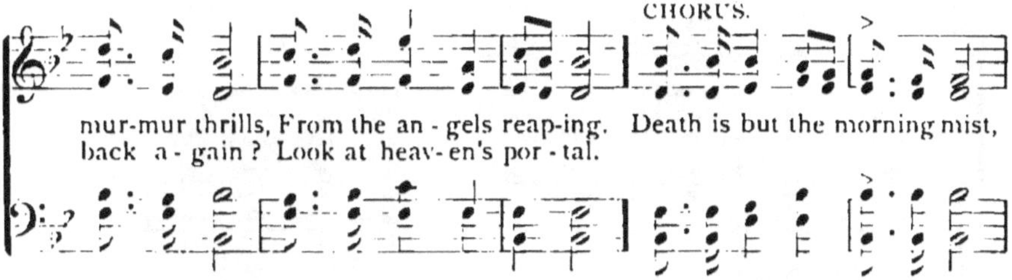

CHORUS.

mur-mur thrills, From the an-gels reap-ing. Death is but the morning mist,
back a-gain? Look at heav-en's por-tal.

Christian, ris-ing o'er thee, Past the hills of am-e-thyst Shines the day of glory.

3 Lift thy tearful eyes in trust,
   Christ, thy treasures keeping,
He who measures earthly dust,
   Human tear-drops weeping.

4 Dost thou fear the open grave,
   Fear death's narrow prison?
Jesus died the lost to save,
   Jesus hath arisen.

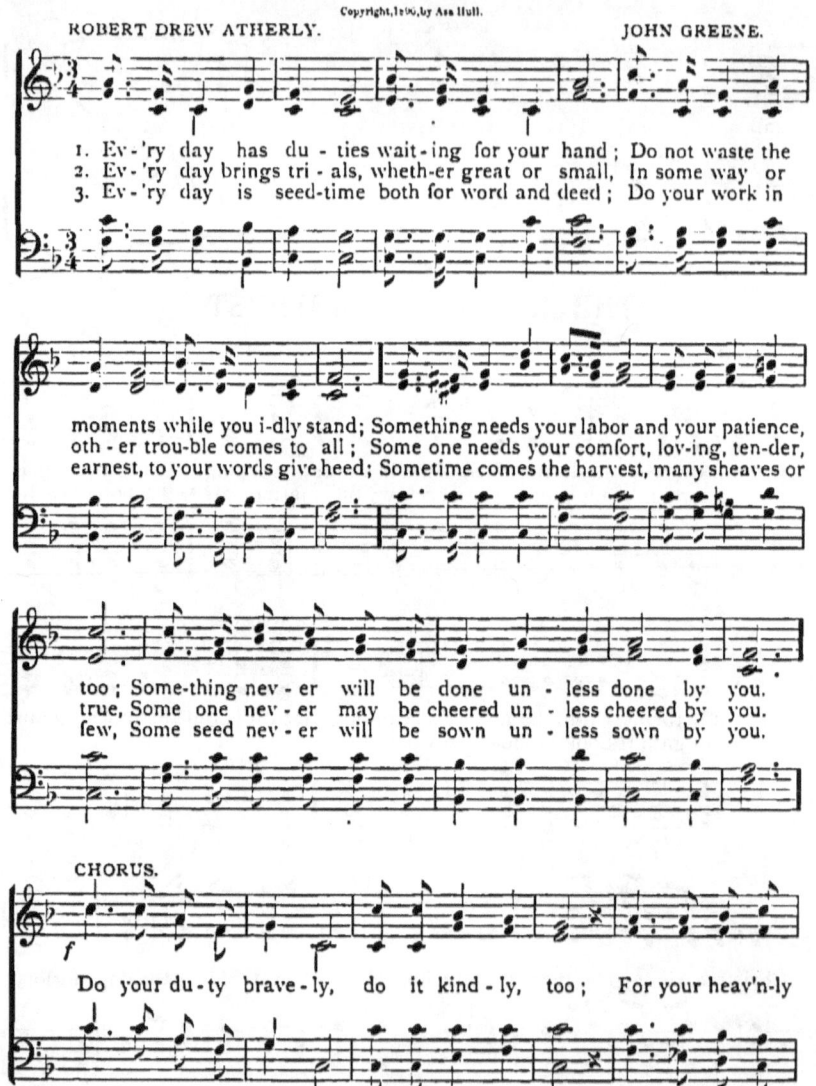

SOMETHING EVERY DAY.—Concluded.

2 Tempt not my soul away;
　Jesus is mine!
　Here would I ever stay;
　Jesus is mine!
　Perishing things of clay,
　Born but for one brief day,
　Pass from my heart away;
　　Jesus is mine!

3 Farewell, ye dreams of night,
　Jesus is mine!
　Lost in this dawning bright,
　Jesus is mine!
　All that my soul has tried
　Left but a dismal void;
　Jesus has satisfied;
　　Jesus is mine!

GOING OUT TO BATTLE—Concluded. 137

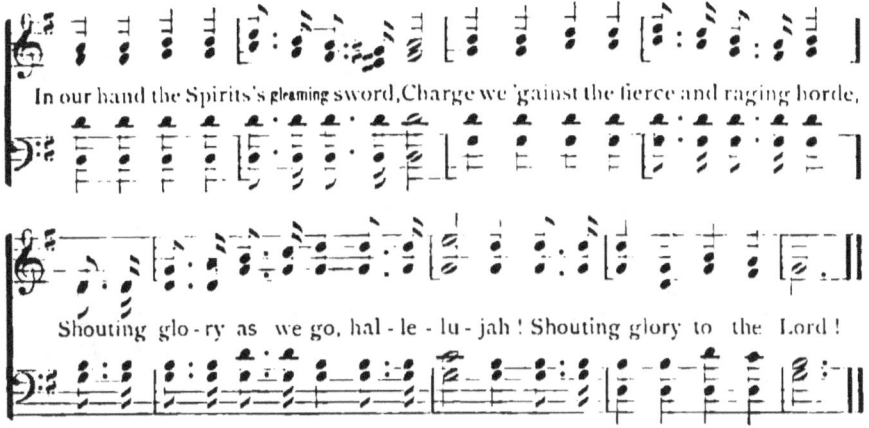

In our hand the Spirits's gleaming sword, Charge we 'gainst the fierce and raging horde,
Shouting glo-ry as we go, hal - le - lu - jah! Shouting glory to the Lord!

OLIVET.

RAY PALMER.   L. MASON.

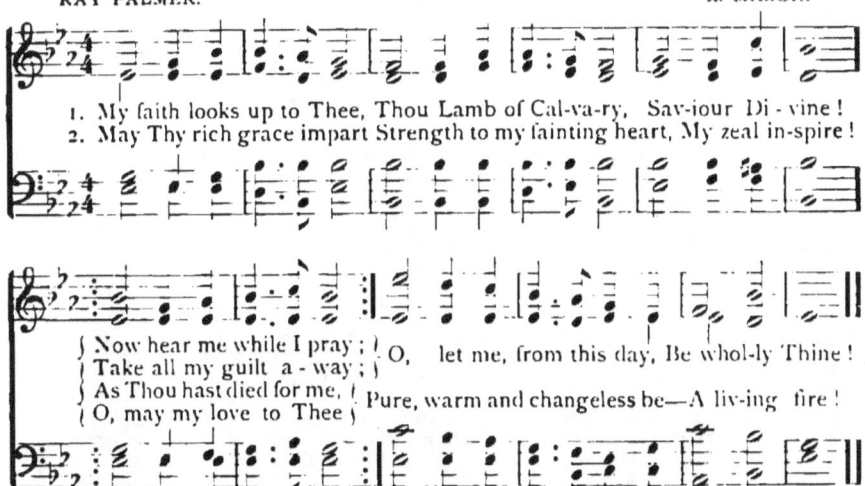

1. My faith looks up to Thee, Thou Lamb of Cal-va-ry, Sav-iour Di - vine!
2. May Thy rich grace impart Strength to my fainting heart, My zeal in-spire!

{ Now hear me while I pray; } O, let me, from this day, Be whol-ly Thine!
{ Take all my guilt a - way; }
{ As Thou hast died for me, } Pure, warm and changeless be—A liv-ing fire!
{ O, may my love to Thee }

3 While life's dark maze I tread,
   And griefs around me spread,
     Be Thou my guide;
   Bid darkness turn to day,
   Wipe sorrow's tears away,
   Nor let me ever stray
     From Thee aside.

4 When ends life's transient dream,
   When death's cold sullen stream
     Shall o'er me roll,
   Blest Saviour! then, in love,
   Fear and distrust remove;
   O, bear me safe above—
     A ransomed soul!

SAIL NOT WITHOUT, Etc.—Concluded.

THE TEMPERANCE BANNER.
(For the foregoing Music.)

1 Unfurl the temp'rance banner,
   And let it proudly wave;
  Let sons and daughters gather
   Fair freedom's land to save.
  From mountain, hill and valley
   Let teeming millions come!
  And round the banner rally,
   Defenders of our home!

 CHO. Then raise the temp'rance banner,
   And let it proudly wave;
  ‖: Let sons and daughters gather
   Fair freedom's land to save! :‖

2 Unfurl the temp'rance banner,
   And let the strong and brave
  Renew the glorious conflict,
   The fallen seek to save;
  And rouse, ye men of valor,
   Be steadfast, firm and true,
  Though long and fierce the battle,
   The vict'ry is for you!

 CHO. Then raise the temp'rance banner,
   And let it proudly wave;
  ‖: Let sons and daughters gather
   Fair freedom's land to save! :‖

Rev. M. L. Hofford.

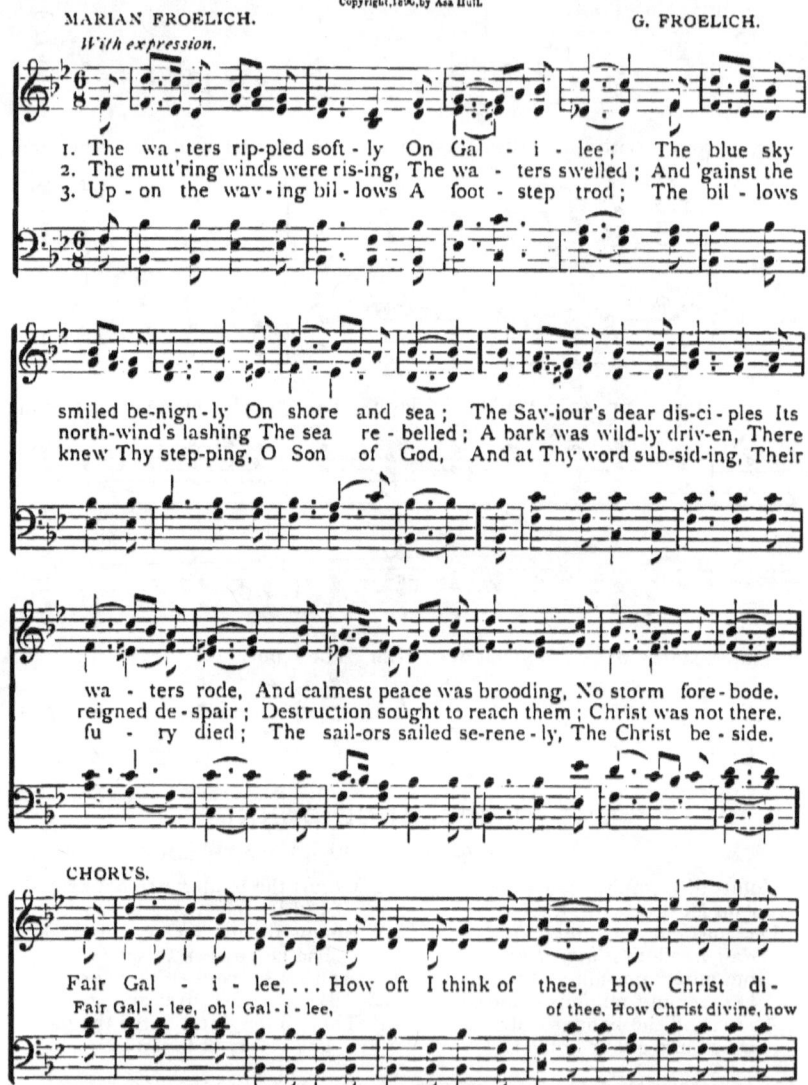

FAIR GALILEE.—Concluded.

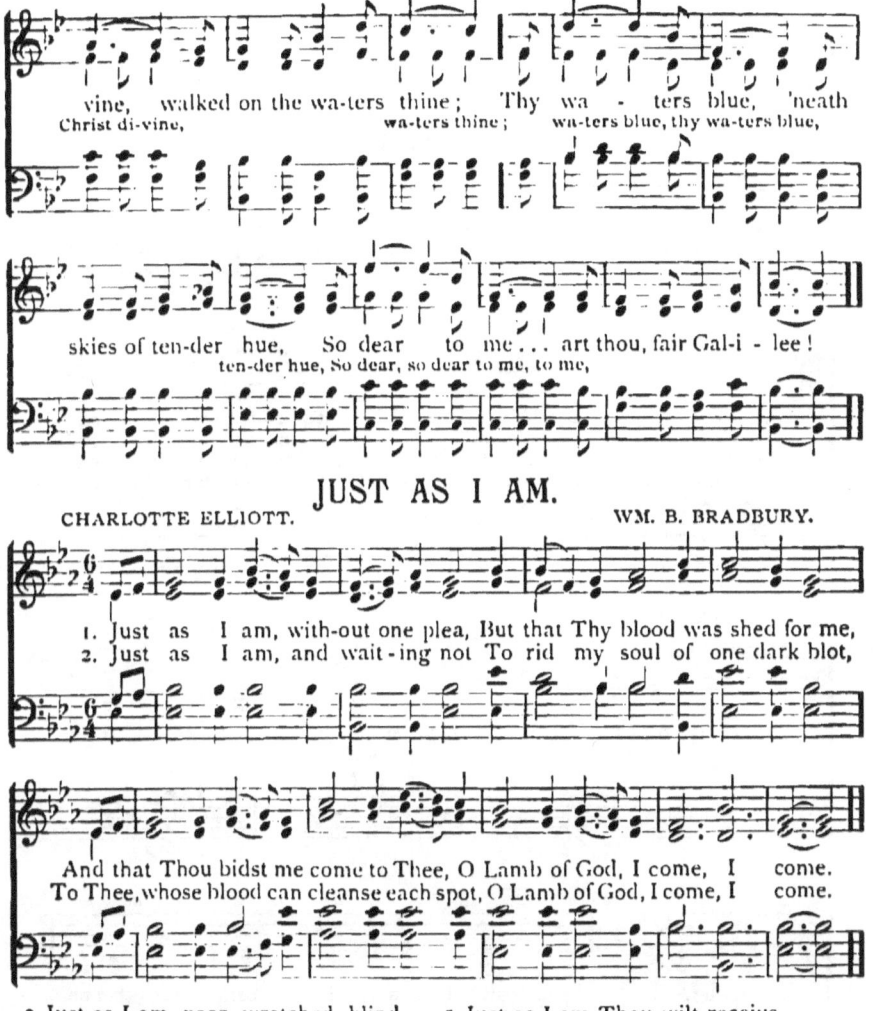

vine, walked on the wa-ters thine; Thy wa - ters blue, 'neath
Christ di-vine, wa-ters thine; wa-ters blue, thy waters blue,

skies of ten-der hue, So dear to me... art thou, fair Gal-i - lee!
ten-der hue, So dear, so dear to me, to me,

JUST AS I AM.

CHARLOTTE ELLIOTT.   WM. B. BRADBURY.

1. Just as I am, with-out one plea, But that Thy blood was shed for me,
2. Just as I am, and wait-ing not To rid my soul of one dark blot,

And that Thou bidst me come to Thee, O Lamb of God, I come, I come.
To Thee, whose blood can cleanse each spot, O Lamb of God, I come, I come.

3. Just as I am, poor, wretched, blind,
Sight, riches, healing of the mind,
Yea, all I need in Thee I find;
   O Lamb of God, I come, I come.

4. Just as I am, though toss'd about,
With many a conflict, many a doubt,
Fightings within, and fears without,—
   O Lamb of God, I come, I come.

5. Just as I am Thou wilt receive,
Wilt welcome, pardon, cleanse, relieve;
Because Thy promise I believe,
   O Lamb of God, I come, I come.

6. Just as I am, Thy love unknown
Hath broken every barrier down;
Now to be Thine, yea, Thine alone,
   O Lamb of God, I come, I come.

YE SOLDIERS OF THE LORD—Concluded.

And when the battle's o'er, And soldiers fight no more,
How sweet to rest when shadows come, And waken in the heav'nly home.

SALVATION'S FREE.

ISAAC WATTS.   C. DUNBAR.

1. Come, ye that love the Lord, And let your joys be known;
Join in a song with sweet accord, While ye surround His throne.
CHO. I'm glad salvation's free, I'm glad salvation's free;
Salvation's free for you and me; I'm glad salvation's free.

2 Let those refuse to sing
   Who never knew our God,
But servants of the heav'nly King
   May speak His praise abroad.

3 There we shall see His face;
   And never, never sin;
There, from the rivers of His grace,
   Drink endless pleasures in.

4 Yea, and before we rise,
   To that immortal state,
The thoughts of such amazing bliss
   Should constant joys create.

5 Then let our songs abound,
   And every tear be dry;
We're marching thro' Immanuel's ground
   To fairer worlds on high.

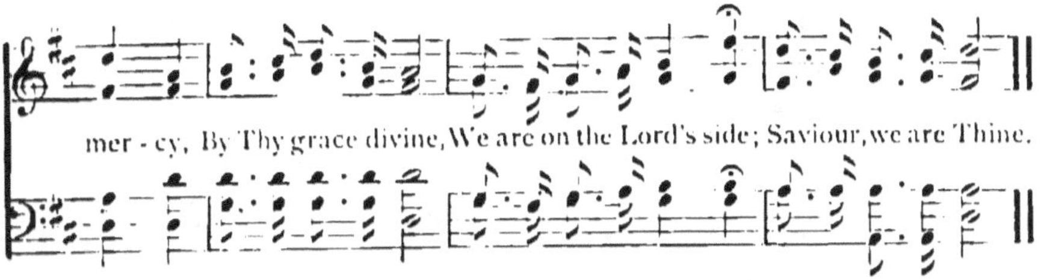

ON THE LORD'S SIDE—Concluded.

mer-cy, By Thy grace divine, We are on the Lord's side; Saviour, we are Thine.

HOLY, LORD GOD ALMIGHTY.

R. HEBER, D.D. REV. JOHN B. DYKES.

1. Ho-ly, Ho-ly, Ho-ly! Lord God Al-might-y! Ear-ly in the
2. Ho-ly, Ho-ly, Ho-ly! all the saints a-dore Thee, Casting down their
3. Ho-ly, Ho-ly, Ho-ly! tho' the darkness hide Thee, Tho' the eye of

morn-ing our songs shall rise to Thee; Ho-ly, Ho-ly, Ho-ly!
gold-en crowns around the glass-y sea; Cher-u-bim and Ser-a-phim
sin-ful man Thy glo-ry may not see, On-ly Thou art Ho-ly,

Mer-ci-ful and Might-y! God in Three Persons, blessed Trin-i-ty.
falling down before Thee, Which wert and art, and evermore shalt be.
there is none be-side Thee Perfect in pow'r, in love, and pu-ri-ty. A-men.

THE OTHER SHORE. Concluded. 149

2. How near it seems, the other shore,
   Where we shall some day gladly rest;
   Where grief and care shall come no more
   Among those hills and valleys blest.
   We sometimes think we see the light
   Reflected from its shining strand,
   And fain would stem life's surging tide
   To reach that fair, unshadowed land.

3. Sweet are the songs that echo there,
   The songs of joy that seraphs sing;
   From out the fadeless hills so fair,
   Sometimes we seem to catch the strain.
   'Twill not be long ere we shall stand
   With loved ones on that happy shore;
   Upon that blissful, golden strand
   We'll rest in peace for evermore!

SOME DAY, YES, SOME DAY.

HARRIET E. JONES.   Copyright, 1891, by Asa Hull.   FRANK M. DAVIS.

1. We shall cross the roll-ing tide, Some day, yes, some day; We shall gain the gold-en side, Some day, yes, some day, O'er those streets of beauty roam, In the saints' eternal home, Where earth's shadows never come, Some day, yes, some day.
2. We shall tread the streets of gold, Some day, yes, some day; Heaven's splendor shall behold, Some day, yes, some day, We shall find the mansions fair, Je-sus promised to prepare, That are wait-ing o-ver there, Some day, yes, some day.
3. We shall join the ransomed throng, Some day, yes, some day; We shall sing re-demption's song, Some day, yes, some day, Un-to Christ the Lord and King, We our gather'd sheaves may bring, In the land where angels sing, Some day, yes, some day.

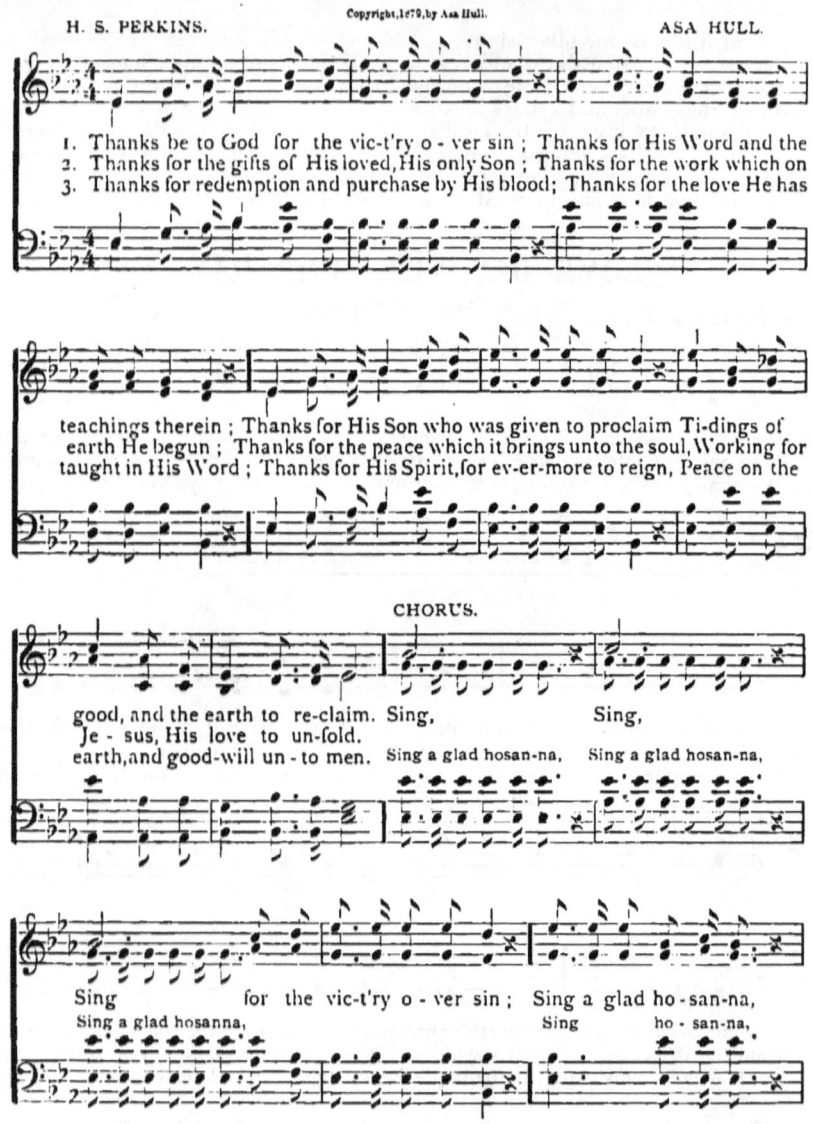

THANKS BE TO GOD—Concluded. 151

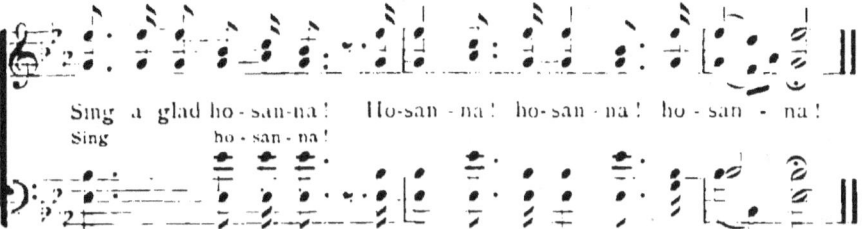

Sing a glad ho-san-na! Ho-san-na! ho-san-na! ho-san-na!
Sing ho-san-na!

WATCHING AT THE DOOR.

CHAS. H. GABRIEL. Copyright, 1891, by Asa Hull. CHAS. H. GABRIEL.

1. Christ is watching at the door, And waits to let me in; Waits to make the
2. He is watching at the door By night and thro' the day; And the latch is
3. He is watching at the door; With all my guilt and shame, He has nev-er
4. Still He's watching at the door; I'll go although 'tis late; Go while mercy's

CHORUS.

heav-y burden light, And wash away my sin! Watching! watching! watching!
al-ways lift-ed high Since I have been a-way.
yet for-got-ten me, Nor blotted out my name.
lamp is burning bright Above the o-pen gate!

Watching there for me! There's a welcome for the prodigal, A welcome there for me.

3 Round each habitation hov'ring,
  See the cloud and fire appear!
  For a glory and a cov'ring,
  Showing that the Lord is near.

4 He who gives us daily manna,
  He who listens when we cry,
  Let Him hear the loud hosanna
  Rising to His throne on high.

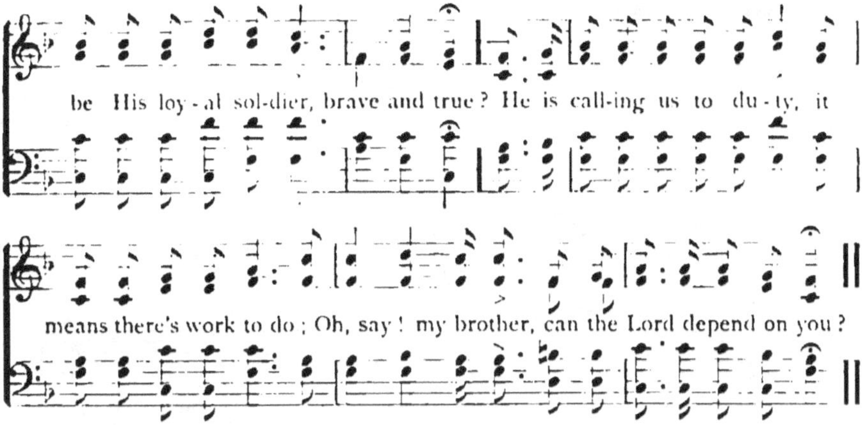

CAN THE LORD DEPEND, Etc.—Concluded.

be His loy-al sol-dier, brave and true? He is call-ing us to du-ty, it
means there's work to do; Oh, say! my brother, can the Lord depend on you?

GLORIA PATRI. No. 1.

ASA HULL.

Copyright, 1887, by Asa Hull.

Glo - ry be to the Fa-ther, and to the Son, and to the
Ho - ly Ghost; As it was in the be-gin-ning, is now, and ev - er
shall be, world with-out end. A-men! A-men! A - men!

JUBILEE YEAR—Concluded. 157

THE MORNING LIGHT IS BREAKING.

S. F. SMITH.   TUNE--WEBB.

1 THE morning light is breaking,
    The darkness disappears;
The sons of earth are waking
    To penitential tears;
Each breeze that sweeps the ocean
    Brings tidings from afar,
Of nations in commotion,
    Prepared for Zion's war.

2 Rich dews of grace come o'er us,
    In many a gentle shower,
And brighter scenes before us,
    Are opening every hour;
Each cry to heaven going
    Abundant answer brings,
And heavenly gales are blowing,
    With peace upon their wings.

3 See heathen nations bending
    Before the God we love,
And thousand hearts ascending
    In gratitude above:
While sinners, now confessing,
    The Gospel-call obey,
And seek the Saviour's blessing,
    A nation in a day.

4 Blest river of salvation,
    Pursue thy onward way;
Flow thou to every nation,
    Nor in thy richness stay:
Stay not till all the lowly
    Triumphant reach their home;
Stay not till all the holy
    Proclaim, "The Lord is come."

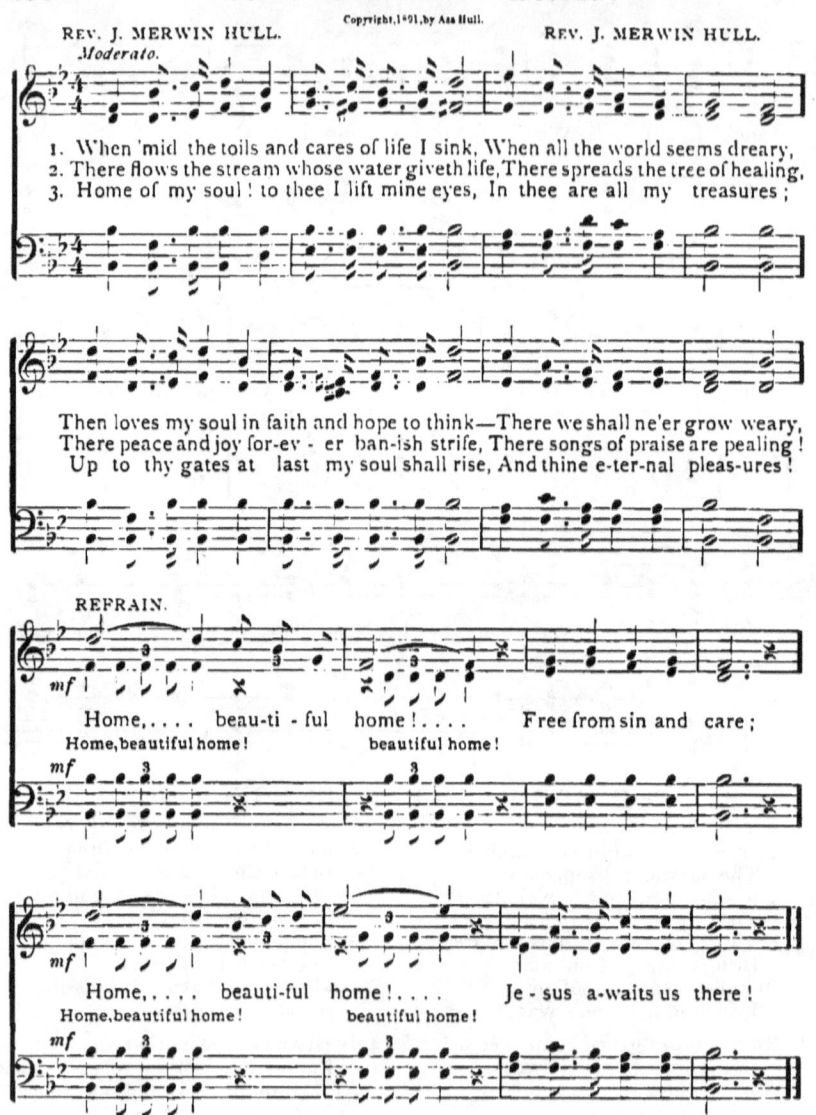

BOUGHT WITH A PRICE.—Concluded.

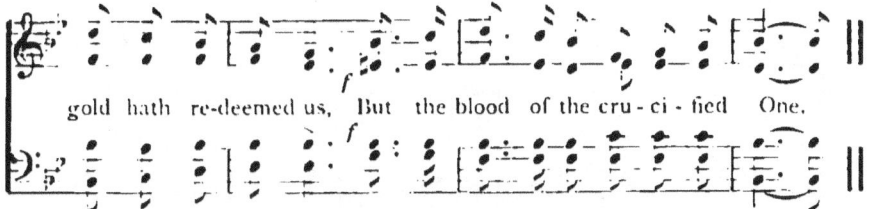

gold hath re-deemed us, But the blood of the cru-ci-fied One.

4 Then the Lord will abundantly pardon,
And your sins be remembered no more,
While your heart will o'erflow with thanksgiving
For unspeakable blessings in store.

DEAR LORD, REMEMBER ME.

Copyright, 1867 & 1896, by Asa Hull.

ISAAC WATTS.   Music and Chorus by ASA HULL.

1. A-las! and did my Sav-iour bleed? And did my Sov-'reign die?
CHO. { Help me dear Sav-iour, Thee to own, And ev-er faith-ful be;
{ Re-mem-ber me, re-mem-ber me, Dear Lord, re-mem-ber me;

Would He de-vote that sa-cred head For such a worm as I?
And when Thou sit-test on Thy throne, Dear Lord, re-mem-ber me.
And when Thou sit-est, etc. (2d part of chorus can be sung or omitted ad. lib.)

2 Was it for crimes that I have done
He groaned upon the tree?
Amazing pity! grace unknown!
And love beyond degree.

3 Well might the sun in darkness hide,
And shut his glory in,
When Christ, the mighty Maker, died
For man, the creature's, sin.

4 Thus might I hide my blushing face
While His dear cross appears;
Dissolve my heart in thankfulness,
And melt mine eyes to tears.

5 But drops of grief can ne'er repay
The debt of love I owe;
Here, Lord, I give myself away,—
'Tis all that I can do.

THE SACRED STREAM—Concluded.

vine .... a - bode, And wa - t'ring our ... di - vine a - bode.
faint - - ing souls, And give new strength to faint - ing souls.
swell - - ing tide, Trem-bles and dreads the swell - ing tide.

GOD SPEED THE RIGHT.

W. E. HICKSON.   GERMAN.

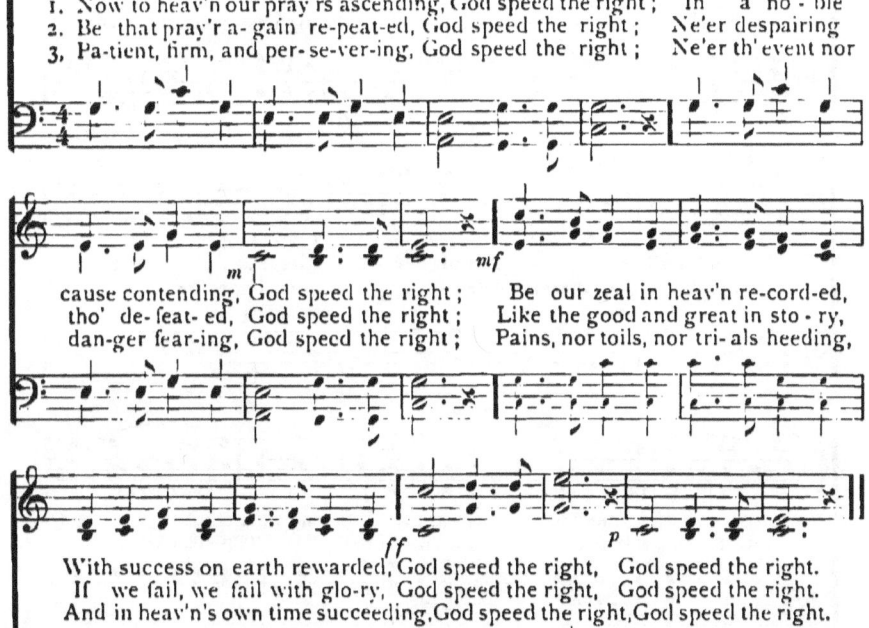

1. Now to heav'n our pray'rs ascending, God speed the right; In a no - ble
2. Be that pray'r a-gain re-peat-ed, God speed the right; Ne'er despairing
3. Pa-tient, firm, and per-se-ver-ing, God speed the right; Ne'er th' event nor

cause contending, God speed the right; Be our zeal in heav'n re-cord-ed,
tho' de-feat-ed, God speed the right; Like the good and great in sto - ry,
dan-ger fear-ing, God speed the right; Pains, nor toils, nor tri - als heeding,

With success on earth rewarded, God speed the right, God speed the right.
If we fail, we fail with glo-ry, God speed the right, God speed the right.
And in heav'n's own time succeeding, God speed the right, God speed the right.

EXCELSIOR—Concluded. 167

never tire,..... For our motto is Excelsior!.....
and never tire, Excelsior!

COME, YE DISCONSOLATE.

T. MOORE. S. WEBBE.

SOLO OR DUET.

DUET, *1st time.* Rep. FULL CHORUS.

1. Come, ye dis-con-so-late, wher-e'er ye lan-guish; Come, at the mer-cy-seat fer-vent-ly kneel; Here bring your wounded hearts, here tell your an-guish, Earth has no sor-row that Heav'n cannot heal.
2. Joy of the des-o-late, light of the stray-ing, Hope of the pen-i-tent, fade-less and pure; Here speaks the Com-fort-er, ten-der-ly say-ing: Earth has no sor-row that Heav'n cannot cure.
3. Here see the Bread of Life; see wa-ters flow-ing Forth from the throne of God, pure from a-bove; Come to the feast of love; come, ev-er knowing. Earth has no sor-row but Heav'n can re-move.

WHAT DO THE BELLS SAY?—Concluded.

BRINGING IN THE SHEAVES.

1 Sowing in the morning, sowing seeds of kindness,
  Sowing in the noontide and the dewy eves;
  Waiting for the harvest, and the time of reaping,
  We shall come rejoicing, bringing in the sheaves.

Cho.—Bringing in the sheaves, bringing in the sheaves,
  We shall come rejoicing, bringing in the sheaves.

2 Sowing in the sunshine, sowing in the shadows,
  Fearing neither clouds nor winter's chilling breeze;
  By and by the harvest, and the labor ended,
  We shall come rejoicing, bringing in the sheaves.

3 Go, then, ever weeping, sowing for the Master,
  Though the loss sustained our spirit often grieves;
  When our weeping's over, He will bid us welcome,
  We shall come rejoicing, bringing in the sheaves.

MARCHING TO THE LAND, Etc.—Concluded. 171

leads us on, March-ing a-long, marching a-long, marching a-long.

CHORUS.

We are marching to the land a-bove, Beau-ti-ful land a-bove,
We are marching t'ward the cit-y fair, Beau-ti-ful cit-y fair,
We are marching to the home of God, Beau-ti-ful home of God,

beau-ti-ful land a-bove; To a land where dwells e-
beau-ti-ful cit-y fair; Where the an-gel an-thems
beau-ti-ful home of God; And our guide-book is His

ter-nal love, Beau-ti-ful land a-bove, land a-bove.
fill the air, Beau-ti-ful cit-y fair, cit-y fair.
ho-ly word, Beau-ti-ful word of God, word of God.

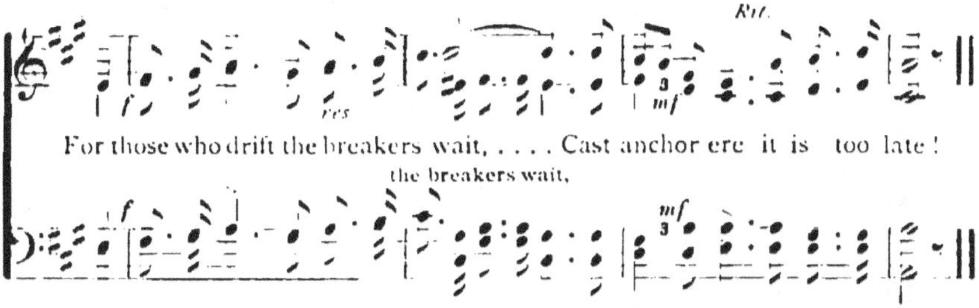

THE ANCHOR OF HOPE.--Concluded.

For those who drift the breakers wait, ... Cast anchor ere it is too late!
the breakers wait,

JESUS, OUR GUIDE.

Miss P. J. OWENS.   Copyright, 1892, by Asa Hull.   JNO. R. BRYANT.

1. We need not wander wide, While pastures green we see; We need not turn a-
2. What can the world bestow, To tempt our hearts astray, When living fountains

CHORUS.

side, When light is shin-ing free! For Je-sus is our Guide, He
flow, To cheer us day by day?

knows our path before, So glad and sat-is-fied, We fol-low ev-er-more.

3 What sorrows can appall
   When Jesus fills the cup?
 Or should we fear and fall
   While Jesus holds us up?

4 Christ is our life and light,
   Our sunshine never dim,
 Our shelter and our might,
   So we will follow Him.

AT THE SETTING OF THE SUN.—Concluded.

4 Then let us still be faithful, though oft our steps be weary,
Nor look behind and loiter, or sigh o'er tasks undone,
But press with vigor onward, all doubtings overcoming,
That He may well reward us at setting of the sun.

WHAT A FRIEND WE HAVE IN JESUS.

1 What a friend we have in Jesus,
All our sins and griefs to bear;
What a privilege to carry
Everything to Him in prayer.
O, what peace we often forfeit,
O, what needless pain we bear;
All because we do not carry
Everything to Him in prayer.

2 Have we trials and temptations?
Is there trouble anywhere?
We should never be discouraged,
Take it to the Lord in prayer.
Can we find a friend so faithful,
Who will all our sorrows share?
Jesus knows our ev'ry weakness,
Take it to the Lord in prayer.

3 Are we weak and heavy-laden,
Cumbered with a load of care,
Precious Saviour, still our refuge,
Take it to the Lord in prayer.
Do thy friends despise, forsake thee,
Take it to the Lord in prayer;
In His arms He'll take and shield thee,
Thou wilt find a solace there.

Dr. H. Bonar.

3 Let music swell the breeze,
   And ring from all the trees
     Sweet freedom's song!
   Let mortal tongues awake;
   Let all that breathe partake;
   Let rocks their silence break;
     The sound prolong!

4 Our father's God! to Thee,
   Author of liberty,
     To Thee we sing:
   Long may our land be bright
   With freedom's holy light;
   Protect us by Thy might,
     Great God, our King!

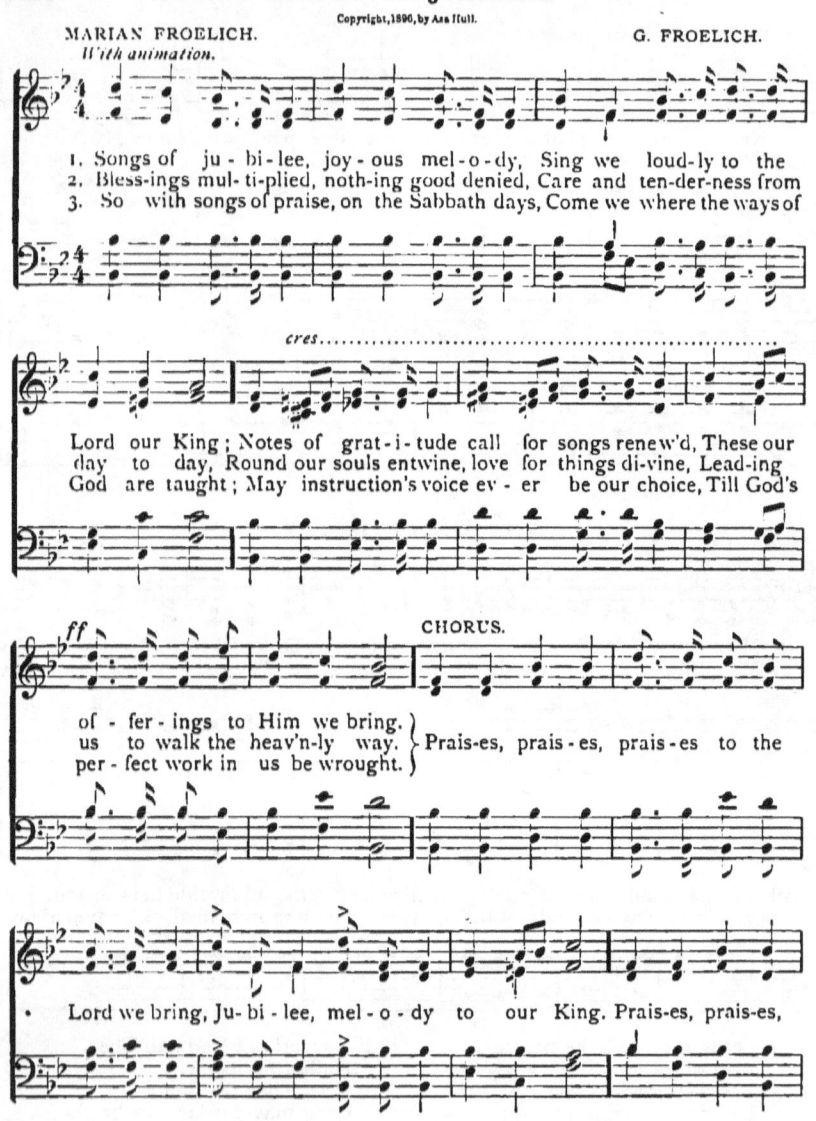

SONGS OF JUBILEE—Concluded.

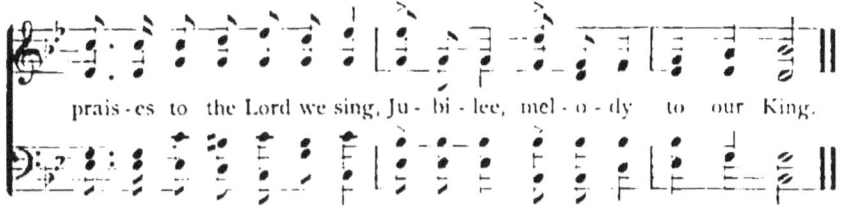

prais-es to the Lord we sing, Ju-bi-lee, mel-o-dy to our King.

O DAY OF REST.

C. WORDSWORTH. GERMAN. ARR. BY L. MASON.

1. { O day of rest and gladness, O day of joy and light! }
   { O balm of care and sadness, Most beau-ti-ful, most bright! }
   On thee, the high and lowly, Before th' e-ter-nal throne,
   Sing Ho-ly! Ho-ly! Ho-ly! To the great Three in One.

2. On thee, at the creation,
    The light first had its birth;
   On thee, for our salvation,
    Christ rose from depths of earth,
   On thee, our Lord, victorious,
    The Spirit sent from heaven,
   And thus on thee most glorious,
    A triple light was given.

3. New graces ever gaining
    From this our day of rest,
   We reach the rest remaining
    To spirits of the blest;
   To Holy Ghost be praises,
    To Father and to Son;
   The Church her voice upraises
    To Thee, blest Three in One.

WE SING THY PRAISE TO-DAY Concluded. 189

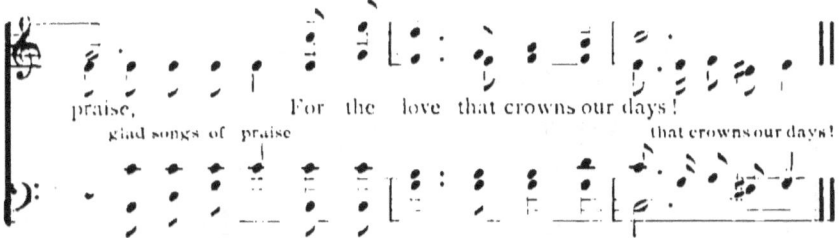

FLAG OF AMERICA.

WM. EDW. PENNEY.
Maestoso.

Copyright, 1898, by Asa Hull.

ASA HULL.

1. Flag of A-mer-i-ca, Em-blem of lib-er-ty, For-ev-er wave! Beau-ti-ful, ev-er bright, Wave in thy peo-ple's might, For freedom, truth, and right, Flag of the brave!
2. Flag of A-mer-i-ca, Sym-bol of u-ni-ty, Of heart and hand; Wher-e'er be-neath the skies, Downtrodden men a-rise, To thee they lift their eyes, And this fair land.
3. Flag of A-mer-i-ca, Brave men have died for thee, On land and sea; Up-on thy star-ry field, Their glo-ry stands re-veal'd, As each new star doth yield, Brightness to thee!

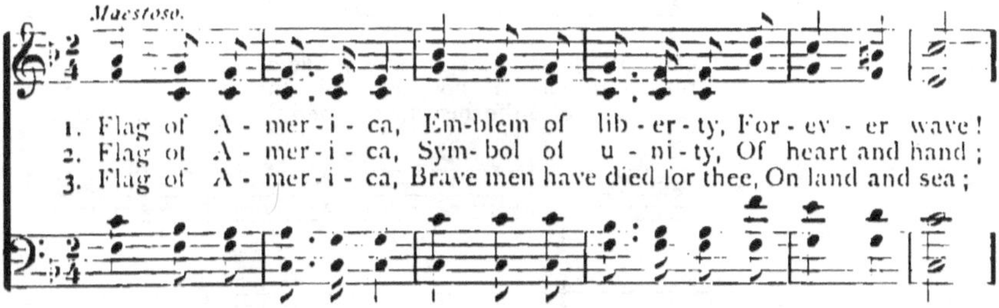

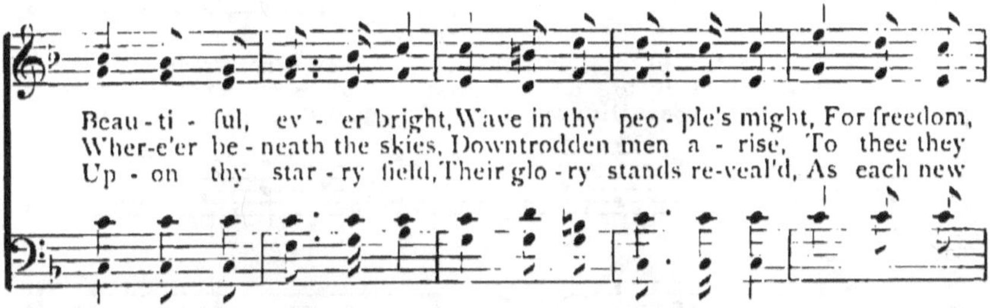

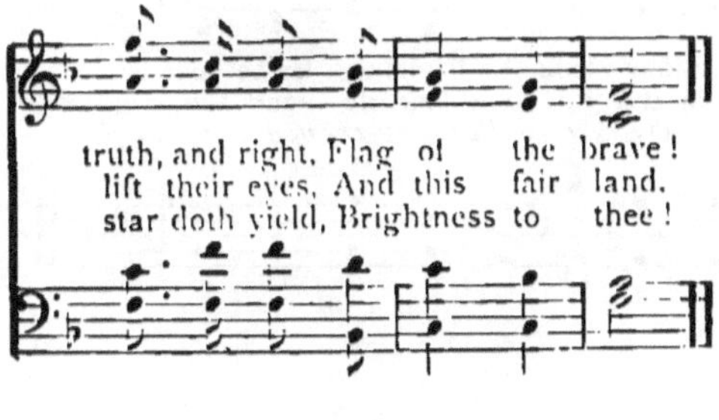

4.
Flag of America,
 Thy people's love for thee,
  What tongue can tell?
Wave to protect and bless,
Wave on for righteousness,
Flag of America,
 God guard thee well!

3 Look up, O trembling mariner,
 Adrift upon the sea,
For Beacon Lights are shining bright,
 To-night to rescue thee.

4 Have faith in God, and falter not ;
 Be trustful and be brave ;
The Beacon Lights are shining bright,
 And Christ is strong to save.

3 Crowns and thrones may perish,
  Kingdoms rise and wane,
But the Church of Jesus
  Constant will remain;
Gates of hell can never
  'Gainst the Church prevail;
We have Christ's own promise,
  And that cannot fail.

4 Onward, then, ye people!
  Join our happy throng,
Blend with ours your voices
  In the triumph-song;
Glory, laud and honor
  Unto Christ, the King;
This through countless ages
  Men and angels sing.

3 Tho' tempests lash the waves to foam,
   No storm shall overwhelm;
   But I shall safely reach my home,
   With Jesus at the helm.

4 My spirit need not feel alarm,
   At all the hosts of sin;
   My ark will shield my soul from harm,
   If I but stay within.

SINGING FOR JESUS. 199

E. RINEHART.
Copyright, 1896, by Asa Hull.
E. RINEHART.

1. Sing-ing for Je-sus all the day long, Sing-ing for Je-sus won-der-ful song;
2. Sing-ing for Je-sus, O what a joy, Sing-ing for Je-sus, bless-ed em-ploy;
3. Sing-ing for Je-sus, Sav-iour di-vine, Sing-ing for Je-sus, Lord, I am Thine;
4. Sing-ing for Je-sus all thro' the night, Sing-ing for Je-sus when it is light;

Trust-ing the full-ness of His love, Jour-ney-ing on to my home a-bove.
Joy of the ran-somed, full and free, O what a bless-ing there comes to me.
O what an o-cean, vast and free, Bound-less His love, for it reach-es me.
Songs of the ran-somed, joy-ful strains, Je-sus, my Sav-iour, for-ev-er reigns.

REFRAIN.

Sing-ing for Je-sus, sing-ing for Je-sus, Sing-ing for Je-sus all the day long;

Sing-ing for Je-sus, bless-ed Re-deem-er, Sing-ing for Je-sus wonderful song!

3 'Twas I that drove the nails,
　And made the thorny crown;
　How can He love me so,
　||: And claim me for His own?" :||

4 Such love has won my heart,
　Blest Saviour, Thou art mine;
　O, take me as I am,
　||: And keep me ever Thine! :||

204. NOT HALF HAS EVER BEEN TOLD.

Rev. J. R. Atchinson.   O. F. Presbrey. By Per.

1. I have read of a beau-ti-ful cit - y,   Far a - way in the kingdom of God;
2. I have read of bright mansions in heaven, Which the Saviour has gone to prepare;

I have read how its walls are of jasper, How its streets are all golden and broad.
And the saints who on earth have been faithful, Rest forever with Christ over there;

In the midst of the street is life's river,   Clear as crystal and pure to be-hold;
There no sin ev-er en-ters, nor sorrow,   The in - hab-i-tants never grow old;

NOT HALF HAS EVER, Etc.—Concluded. 205

3 I have read of white robes for the righteous,
    Of bright crowns which the glorified wear,
  When our Father shall bid them "Come, enter,
    And my glory eternally share;"
  How the righteous are evermore blessed
    As they walk through the streets of pure gold;
  But not half of the wonderful story To mortals, etc.

4 I have read of a Christ so forgiving,
    That vile sinners may ask and receive
  Peace and pardon from every transgression,
    If when asking they only believe.
  I have read how He'll guide and protect us,
    If for safety we'll enter His fold;
  But not half of His goodness and mercy To mortals, etc.

OVER AND OVER AGAIN—Concluded.

I must take my turn at the mill, I must grind out the gold-en grain, I must do my task with a res-o-lute will, O-ver and o-ver a-gain.

THE GREAT PHYSICIAN.

Arr. by ASA HULL.   Rev. J. H. STOCKTON.

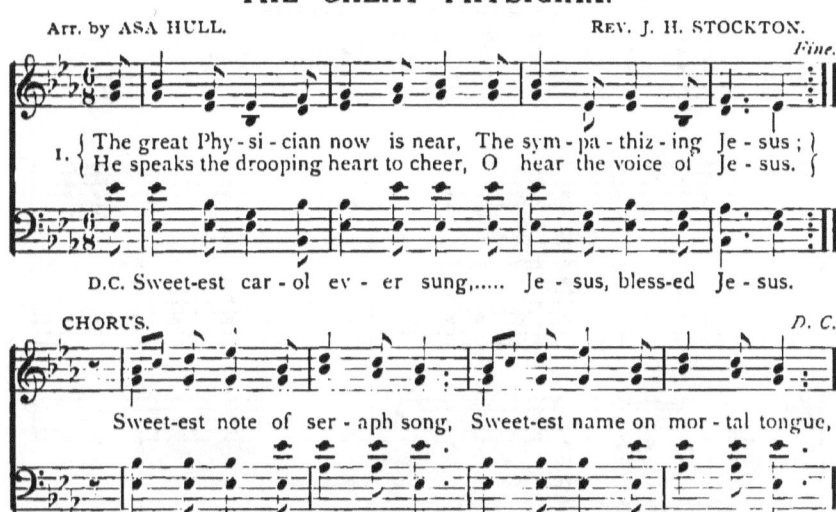

1. The great Phy-si-cian now is near, The sym-pa-thiz-ing Je-sus;
   He speaks the drooping heart to cheer, O hear the voice of Je-sus.

D.C. Sweet-est car-ol ev-er sung,...... Je-sus, bless-ed Je-sus.

CHORUS.

Sweet-est note of ser-aph song, Sweet-est name on mor-tal tongue,

2 Your many sins are all forgiven,
  O, hear the voice of Jesus;
  Go on your way in peace to heaven,
  And wear a crown with Jesus.

3 All glory to the dying Lamb!
  I now believe in Jesus;

  I love the blessed Saviour's name,
  I love the name of Jesus.

4 And when to that bright world above,
  We rise to see our Jesus,
  We'll sing around the throne of love
  His name, the name of Jesus.

OUR FESTAL DAY—Concluded.

A-gain.... we sing,... we sing our cheer-ful lay!...
a-gain we sing, we sing, cheer-ful lay!
And praise the Lord who made the flow'rs That glad-den us to-day!

CLINGING TO THE SAVIOUR.

Rev. E. H. Nevin.   Asa Hull.

1. O, let me cling to Thee, My Saviour, cling to Thee! When I'm weak and weary,
2. O, let me cling to Thee, My Saviour, cling to Thee! When the winds are blowing,
And my path is drear-y; O, let me cling to Thee, My Saviour, cling to Thee.
And my tears are flowing; O, let me cling to Thee, My Saviour, cling to Thee.

3 O, let me cling to Thee, etc.
  When my friends are leaving,
  And my heart is grieving;
  O, let me cling to Thee, etc.

4 O, let me cling to Thee, etc.
  When I cross the river,
  Which from earth doth sever,
  O, let me cling to Thee, etc.

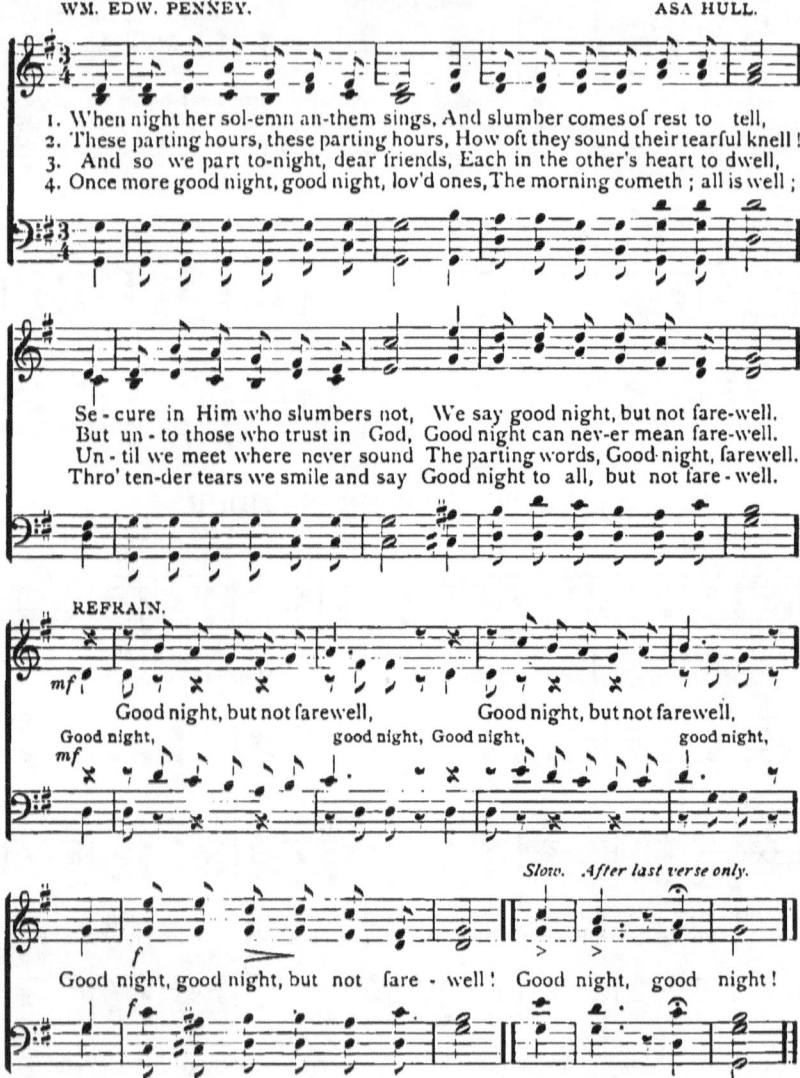

GOD BE WITH YOU.

211

Rev. J. E. RANKIN, D.D.   W. G. TOMER. By Per

1. God be with you till we meet again ! By His counsels guide, uphold you,
2. God be with you till we meet again ! 'Neath His wings securely hide you,
3. God be with you till we meet again ! When life's perils thick confound you,
4. God be with you till we meet again ! Keep love's banner floating o'er you,

With His sheep secure-ly fold you ; God be with you till we meet a-gain !
Dai - ly man-na still provide you; God be with you till we meet a-gain !
Put His loving arms a-round you ! God be with you till we meet a-gain !
Smite death's threat'ning wave before you ; God be with you till we meet a-gain !

CHORUS.

Till we meet ! till we meet ! Till we meet at Je - sus' feet !
Till we meet ! till we meet again !   till we meet !

Till we meet ! till we meet ! God be with you till we meet a-gain !
Till we meet ! till we meet a-gain !

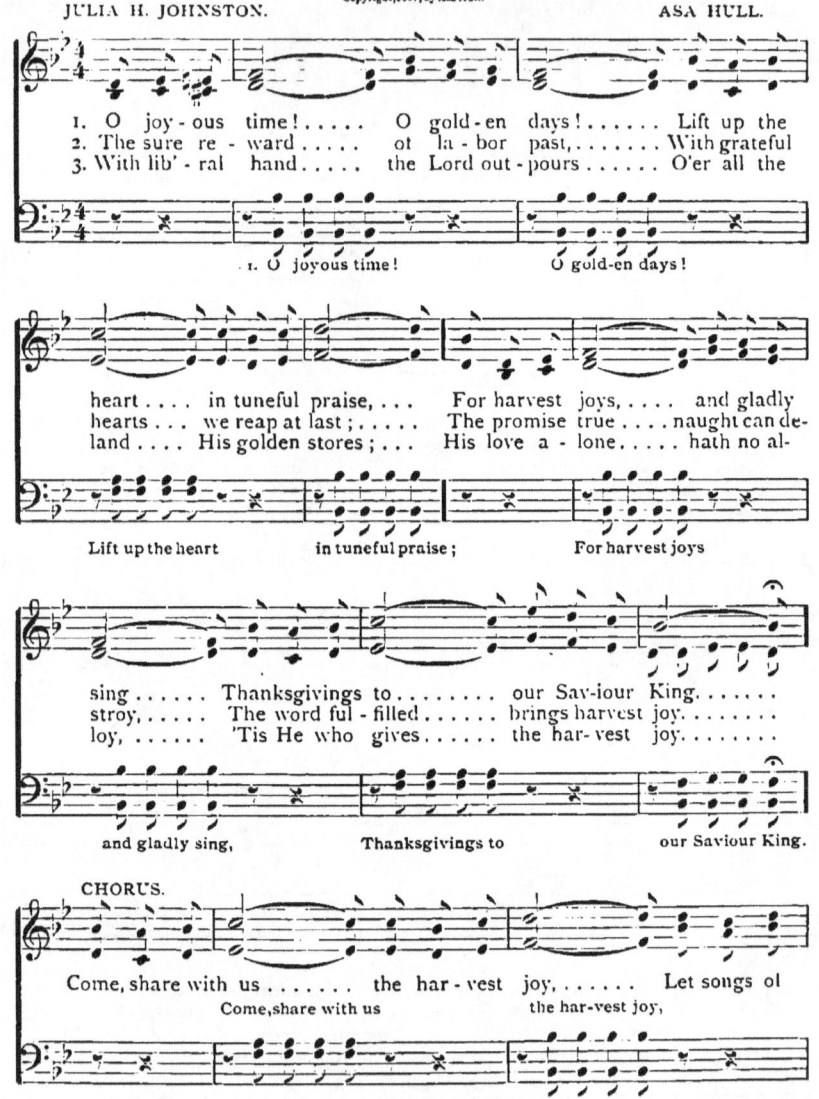

THE SHEAF-BEARERS—Concluded.

MANOAH.

CHARLES WESLEY.   HAYDN.

1. Oh, for a heart to praise my God, A heart from sin set free,—
A heart that al-ways feels Thy blood, So free-ly spilt for me.

2. A heart re-sign'd, sub-mis-sive, meek, My great Re-deem-er's throne,
Where on-ly Christ is heard to speak: Where Je-sus reigns a-lone.

3 Oh, for a lowly, contrite heart,
   Believing, true, and clean,
Which neither life nor death can part,
From Him that dwells within :—

4 A heart in every thought renewed,
   And full of love divine ;
Perfect, and right, and pure, and good,
   A copy, Lord, of Thine.

216. THANKS TO THEE, OUR FATHER.

HARRIET E. JONES. ASA HULL.

3 For the many-colored flowers,
   For the pretty woodland bowers,
   For the peaceful summer hours,
     Thanks to Thee, our Father.

4 For the beauty everywhere,
   For the friends our joys to share,
   For Thy constant love and care,
     Thanks to Thee, our Father.

* The Basses can sing "Thanks" softly as accompaniment for first three lines, or the words all through if preferred.

THANKSGIVING HYMN.

3. For the sunshine and the showers
   That have wrought this grand display;
   For the grain, and fruits delicious,
   Let us keep Thanksgiving day.

4. For the friends that still are left us,
   And for hope's inspiring ray,
   With glad hearts, and sunny faces,
   Let us keep this festal day.

PRAISE THE LORD.—Concluded.

A CHARGE TO KEEP I HAVE.

Tune, Boylston.

1 A charge to keep I have,
  A God to glorify,
  A never-dying soul to save,
  And fit it for the sky.

2 To serve the present age,
  My calling to fulfill;
  O, may it all my powers engage
  To do my Master's will.

3 Arm me with jealous care,
  As in Thy sight to live;
  And O, Thy servant, Lord, prepare
  A strict account to give.

4 Help me to watch and pray,
  And on Thyself rely,
  Assured, if I my trust betray,
  I shall forever die.

CHRISTMAS THOUGHTS—Concluded.

CHORUS.

Al-le-lu-iah! Al-le-lu-iah! Hail God's wondrous gift to man!
Al-le-lu-iah! Al-le-lu-iah! Praise Him for re-demption's plan!
Al-le-lu — — — iah! Al-le-lu — — — iah!
Al-le-lu-iah! Al-le-lu-iah!

THE HERALD ANGELS.

CHARLES WESLEY.   ASA HULL.

1. Hark! the her-ald an-gels sing, "Glo-ry to the new-born King!"
2. Joy-ful, all ye na-tions, rise; Join the tri-umph of the skies!

Peace on earth, and mer-cy mild, God and sin-ners rec-on-ciled,
With th'an-gel-ic host pro-claim, Christ is born in Beth-le-hem.

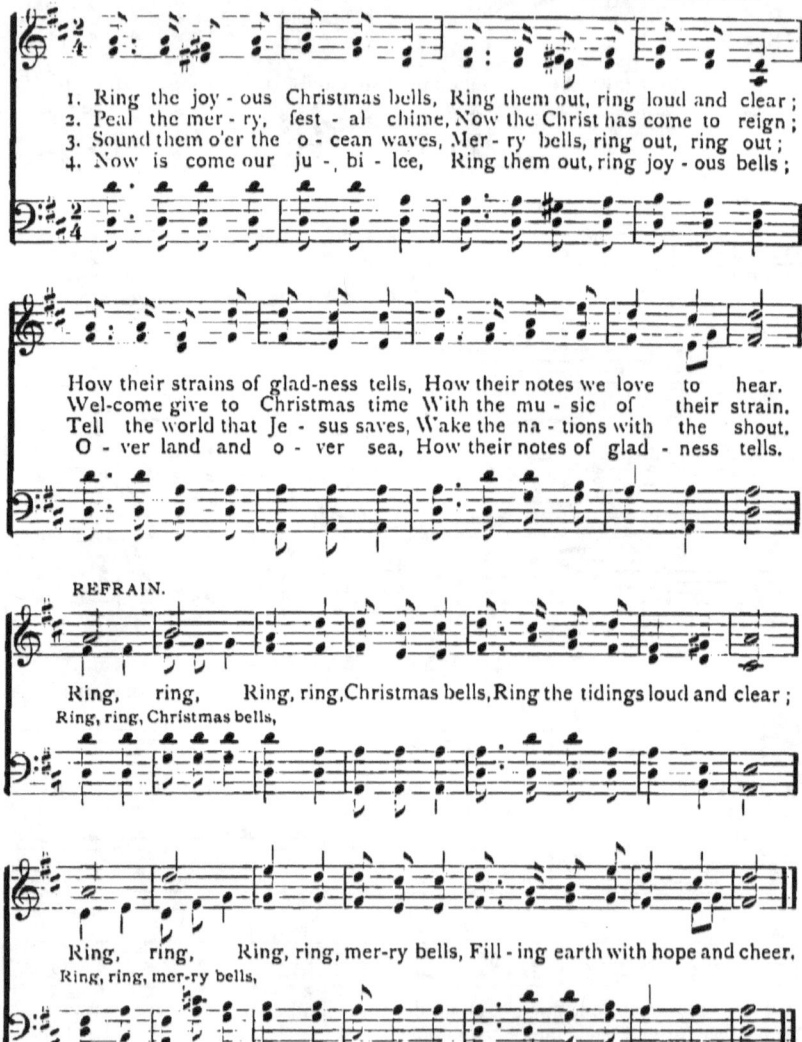

RING OUT THE BELLS—Concluded.

MARTYN.

C. WESLEY. S. B. MARSH. ARR.

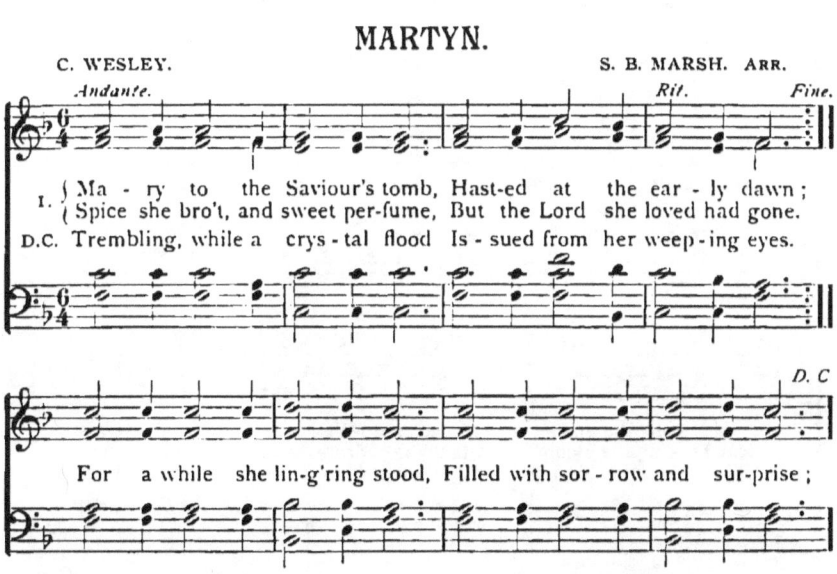

1. Ma-ry to the Saviour's tomb, Hast-ed at the ear-ly dawn;
Spice she bro't, and sweet per-fume, But the Lord she loved had gone.
D.C. Trembling, while a crys-tal flood Is-sued from her weep-ing eyes.

For a while she lin-g'ring stood, Filled with sor-row and sur-prise;

2 But her sorrow quickly fled,
  When she heard His welcome voice;
  Christ had risen from the dead;
  Now He bids her heart rejoice.

What a change His word can make,
  Turning darkness into day!
  Ye who weep for Jesus' sake,
  He will wipe your tears away.

228 GOLDEN BELLS.

W. H. RUDDIMAN.
Copyright, 1879, by Asa Hull.
W. J. KIRKPATRICK.

1. Welcome to the merry, merry Christmas time, Gladsome with melodious flow;
2. Welcome to the merry, merry Christmas time, Teeming with good-will to man;
3. Happy be our greetings to the Christmas time, Brighter than with Bethl'hem's star,

Send-ing out the mu-sic of its hopes sublime, Charming all the earth below.
Sweet as with the o-dors of an E-den clime, Chief in God's redeeming plan.
O'er the world rejoicing sounds its richest chime, Now its splendors blaze afar;

Day of heav'n's im-part-ed peace, May we feel thy joys di-vine in-crease;
Man's sal-va-tion is thy cheer, Thou hast banished sin's en-slaving fear,
See the dead come forth to life, And the reign of love o'er-master strife;

Catching still the beams of that clear morn When our Infant Lord was born.
Scat-ter-ing the gloom be-neath thy ray, From the Saviour's na-tal day.
Glo-ry in the high-est be the song Un-to God from ev-'ry tongue.

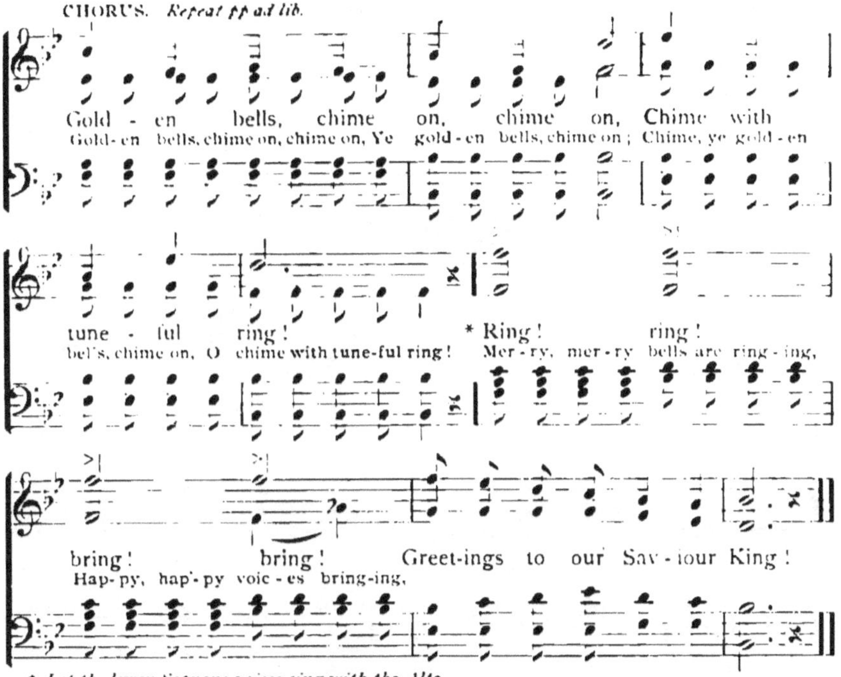

GOLDEN BELLS—Concluded.

* Let the lower Soprano voices sing with the Alto.

OLD HUNDRED. Doxology.

Praise God, from whom all blessings flow; Praise Him, all creatures here below;

Praise Him a-bove, ye heav'nly host; Praise Father, Son, and Ho-ly Ghost.

CHRISTMAS BELLS ARE RINGING Concluded. 231

Peal-ing out the sto - ry, swing-ing to and fro;....

Hap-py chil-dren's voic-es sing the glad re-frain...

Rit. ad lib.

Of the In-fant Sav-iour, born in Beth-le-hem.....

BETHLEHEM'S STAR.

H. K. WHITE.   ASA HULL.

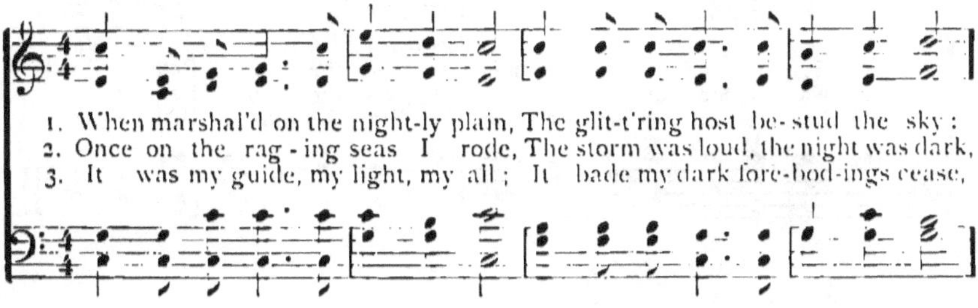

1. When marshal'd on the night-ly plain, The glit-t'ring host be-stud the sky:
2. Once on the rag-ing seas I rode, The storm was loud, the night was dark,
3. It was my guide, my light, my all; It bade my dark fore-bod-ings cease,

SWELL THE STRAIN Concluded.

COMING TO THE CROSS.

1 I am coming to the cross ;
   I am poor, and weak, and blind ;
   I am counting all but dross ;
   I shall full salvation find.

Cho.—I am trusting, Lord in Thee,
   Dear Lamb of Calvary ;
   Humbly at Thy cross I bow ;
   Save me, Jesus, save me now.

2 Long my heart has sighed for Thee ;
   Long has evil reigned within ;
   Jesus sweetly speaks to me,
   I will cleanse you from all sin.

3 Here I give my all to Thee,—
   Friends, and time, and earthly store;
   Soul and body Thine to be—
   Wholly Thine—for evermore.

4 In the promises I trust ;
   Now I feel the blood applied ;
   I am prostrate in the dust ;
   I with Christ am crucified.

5 Jesus comes ! He fills my soul !
   Perfected in love I am ;
   I am every whit made whole ;
   Glory, glory to the Lamb.

EASTER OFFERINGS—Concluded.

CHRIST IS RISEN TO-DAY.

CHAS. WESLEY. CHAS. ZEUNER.

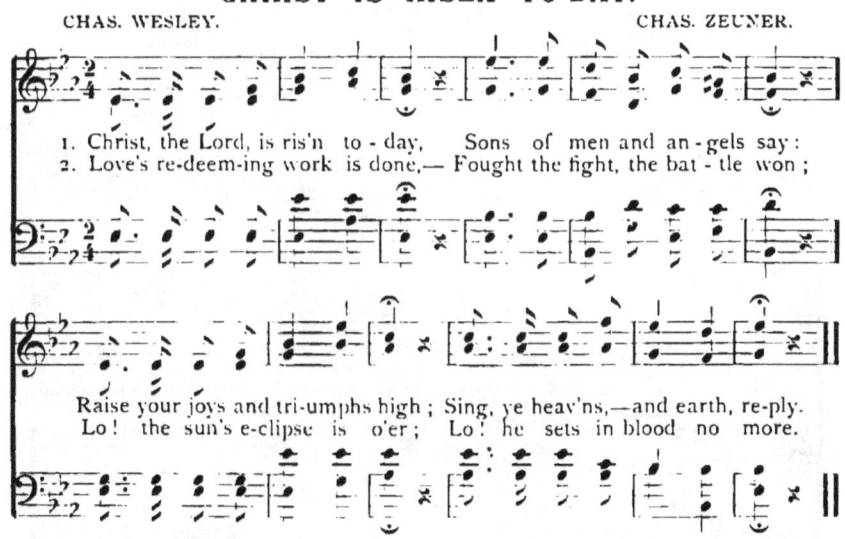

1. Christ, the Lord, is ris'n to-day, Sons of men and an-gels say:
Raise your joys and tri-umphs high; Sing, ye heav'ns,—and earth, re-ply.

2. Love's re-deem-ing work is done,— Fought the fight, the bat-tle won;
Lo! the sun's e-clipse is o'er; Lo! he sets in blood no more.

3 Vain the stone, the watch, the seal;
Christ has burst the gates of hell;
Death in vain forbids His rise;
Christ hath opened Paradise.

4 Lives again our glorious King;
Where, O death, is now thy sting?
Once He died our souls to save;
Where's thy vict'ry, boasting grave?

THE MASTER IS RISEN.—Concluded.

But we look for the signs of His liv - ing In the hearts of the children of men.
And truth wins a soul or a king - dom The Mas-ter is ris - en in - deed!
Be-hind are the grave and the darkness, The Mas-ter is ris - en in - deed!

THE LORD AROSE.

ELIZA M. SHERMAN.
Copyright, 1888, by Asa Hull.
ASA HULL.

1. It came up - on the ear - ly morn, That voice so sweet and clear;
2. He suf-fer'd death for ev - 'ry - one, He suf - fer'd in our stead;
3. O an-gels, we would join the song, And glo - ry, glo - ry sing,

Why seek the liv-ing 'mong the dead? The Sav-iour is not here!
But now the vic - to - ry is won, He's ris - en from the dead.
In tri - umph to our ris - en Lord, Our Sav-iour and our King!

REFRAIN.

"The Lord is ris'n," the an-gels say, The Lord a-rose this Eas-ter day.

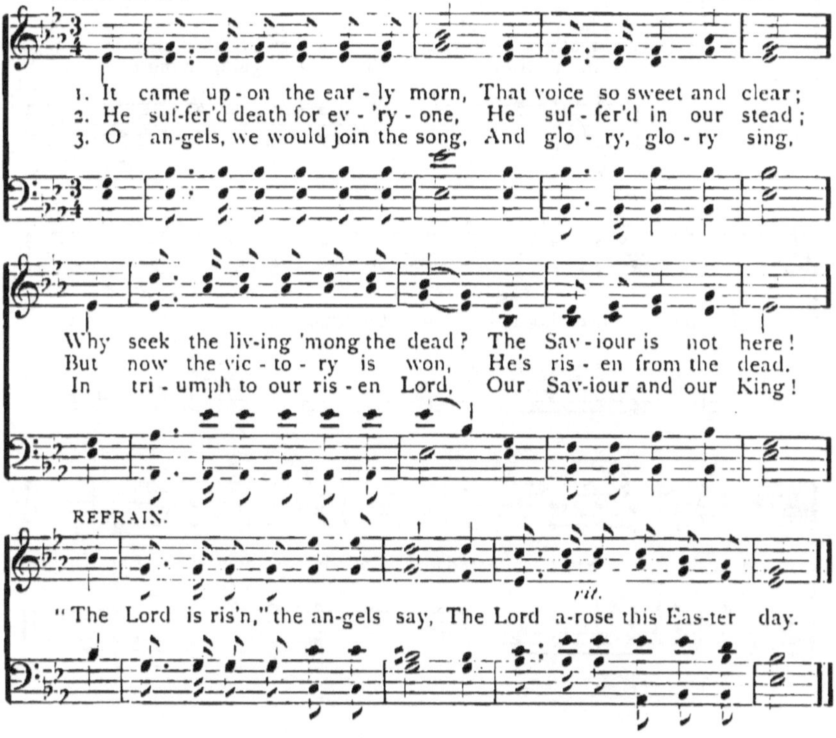

244 GLAD HOSANNAS.

H. S. THURSBY.   Copyright, 1898, by Asa Hull.   R. L. FLETCHER.

1. Ho - san - na! let the na-tions sing, Ho - san-na raise to Christ our King;
2. Let an - gel harps find blest employ, And earth re-peat her new found joy;
3. A world redeemed shall sing His praise, All nature, too, her anthems raise;
4. With hal - le-lu-jahs praise His name, Till earth shall ring with glad acclaim;

The broken seal, the sundered tomb, Dis-pels the night of death and gloom.
The Prince of Life, with pow'r to save, In might is ris - en from the grave.
The perfumed breath of lil - ies fair, A ris - en Christ to men de-clare.
Ho - san - nas sing to Him on high, Who lives a-gain, no more to die.

REFRAIN.

Ho - san-nas raise, ho-san-nas sing, Let praise to Him un-ceas-ing ring;

Our Saviour rose o'er conquered foes, And liv - eth now for-ev - er King!

A HAPPY NEW YEAR—Concluded.

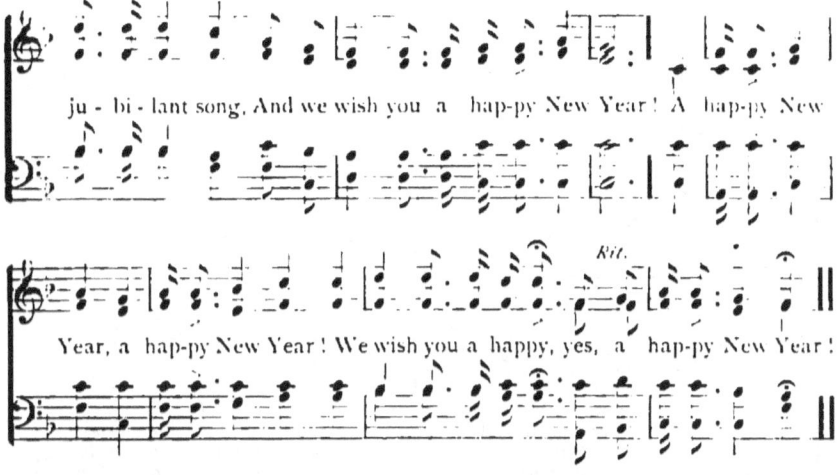

ju-bi-lant song, And we wish you a hap-py New Year! A hap-py New Year, a hap-py New Year! We wish you a happy, yes, a hap-py New Year!

SUN OF MY SOUL.

J. KEBLE. F. J. HAYDN.

1. Sun of my soul, Thou Sav-iour dear, It is not night if Thou be near;
2. When the soft dews of kind-ly sleep My wea-ried eye-lids gen-tly steep,

O, may no earth-born cloud a-rise To hide Thee from Thy servant's eyes.
Be my last thought, how sweet to rest For-ev-er on my Saviour's breast.

3 Abide with me from morn till eve,
For without Thee I cannot live;
Abide with me when death is nigh,
For without Thee I dare not die.

4 If some poor wandering child of Thine
Has spurned to-day the voice divine—
Now, Lord, the gracious work begin;
Let him no more lie down in sin.

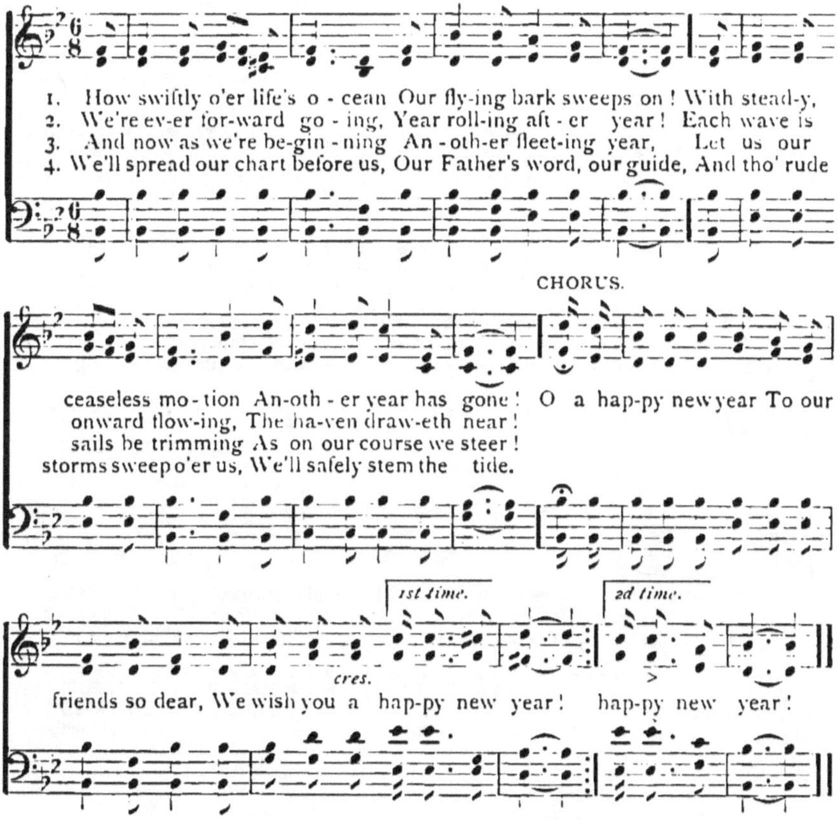

THE BOOK OF THE NEW YEAR.

CHAS. EDW. POLLOCK.

1. The book of the New Year is o-pen'd, Its pag-es are spotless and new;
2. And weave for your souls a fair garment Of hon-or and beaut-y and truth,
3. And if on a page you dis-cov-er At ev-'ning a blot or a scrawl,

And so as each leaf-let is turn-ing, Dear scholars, beware what you do!
Which will with a glo-ry en-fold you, When fades the sweet visions of youth;
Kneel quickly and ask the dear Sav-iour In mer-cy to cov-er it all;

Let nev-er a bad thought be cherish'd, Ab-stain from a whisper of guile;
And now, with the new book, endeavor To write its white pages with care;
So, when the strange book shall be finish'd, And closed by the angel of light,

And see that your faces are windows, Thro' which a sweet spirit shall smile.
Each day is a leaf-let, re-mem-ber, To be written with watching and pray'r.
You'll feel, tho' the work is imperfect, You've tried to please God in the right.

INDEX OF TITLES.

Title	Page
A happy New Year	248
Aim high	122
All for Jesus (male voices)	129
All for Jesus (mixed voices)	131
Always True	56
At the Pool of Siloam	80
At the Setting of the Sun	178
Battling for Temperance	105
Beacon Lights are Shining	193
Be ready and obey	112
Bethlehem's Star	231
Better further on	142
Be up and doing	62
Beyond the Gates	116
Beyond the Shadows	86
Blessed is He that cometh	220
Blest be the Tie	61
Bought with a Price	162
Buds and Blossoms	100
Call to Prayer	182
Can the Lord depend on you?	154
Carol the Christmas Song	225
Christ is risen to-day	241
Christ the Burden-bearer	191
Christmas	91
Christmas Bells	224
Christmas Bells are ringing	230
Christmas Music	233
Christmas Thoughts	222
Clinging to the Saviour	209
Come!	43
Come, ye Disconsolate	167
Crown Him forever	128
Crown Him Lord of all	50
Crowned with Praise	3
Dear Lord, remember me	163
Easter Offerings	240
Echoes from Bethlehem	192
Echoed Songs	4
E'en as a Bird	44
Even me	123
Eventide	177
Excelsior	166
Fairer than Sharon's Rose	102
Fair Galilee	140
Flag of America	189
For God and Country	245
Forget me not	69
Fount for Cleansing	20
From o'er the Sea	68
Gathering Home	18
Glad Hosannas	244
Gloria Patri, No. 1	155
Gloria Patri, No. 2	181
Glorious Easter Day	89
God be with you	211
God speed the Right	165
God's wondrous Love	83
Going out to Battle	136
Golden Bells	228
Good-bye, good-bye	109
Good Night, but not Farewell	210
Go tell it to Jesus	36
Grace divine and free	35
Hail the Risen King	239
Harvest Thanksgiving	213
Harwell	51
Help a Little	28
He's the Best of all	9
Hide me, Saviour	25
His Guiding Hand	111
Ho, every One that thirsteth	60
Holy, Lord God Almighty	147
Hour of Prayer	19
I am going to be crowned	14
I'm on my Journey Home	29
In Gladness, we come	15
In sweet By-and-by	85
In the Cross of Christ	67
In the King's Highway	106
In the Wilderness	120
In Well-doing, be not weary	12
Is your Heart all cleansed?	77
Italian Hymn	57
It all will be Bright	74
Jesus calls for Workers	132
Jesus is coming again	88
Jesus is mine	135
Jesus knows all about it	38
Jesus on the Sea	118
Jesus, our Guide	173
Jesus, Saviour, pilot me	65
Jesus, Shepherd, lead us	11
Joyous Children's Day	101
Jubilee Year	156
Just a little Sunshine	108
Just as I am	141
Labor for the Master	40
Land of the Free	247
Lead, kindly Light	143

INDEX OF TITLES.

Title	PAGE
Let the King come in	22
Let the Light shine in	17
Let Thy Mercy shine on me	183
Life's flowing River	115
Life's onward March	8
Light	64
Loyalty to the Master	66
Manoah	215
Marching to the Land above	170
Martyn	227
Mercy's Free	153
Move Forward	13
My blessed Redeemer	76
My Name	119
National Hymn	185
'Neath the Banner glorious	32
New Year Greeting	251
Not Half has ever been told	204
O Day of Rest	187
Oh, be ready	24
Old Hundred—Doxology	229
Olivet	137
One Day nearer Home	184
Only ask, believing	31
Only remembered	200
On the Lord's Side	146
Onward, Christian Soldiers	195
Onward, right onward	99
O Shepherd, 'tis only One	176
Our Festal Day	208
Our Native Land	246
Over and over again	206
Over to Beulah Land	124
Pass the Word along	26
Praise the King	125
Praise the Lord	218
Praise waiteth for Thee	212
Put on the whole Armor	72
Reaping where thou hast not Sown	16
Response—After Prayer	221
Response—Glory to God	235
Resting in the Sunlight	175
Resting, sweetly resting	130
Ring out the Bells	226
Rock of Ages	47
Sail not without the Master	138
Salvation's Free	145
Save and comfort me	107
Shield me, Father	5
Singing for Jesus	199
Sing on, sing sweetly on	160
Softly now the Light of Day	53
Soldier of the Cross	159
Some Day, yes some Day	149
Something every Day	134
Songs of Jubilee	186
Sow and gather	98
So will I comfort thee	41
Stand Firm	126
Standing for the Good and Right	23
Stand up for Jesus	194
Stop a Moment and think	198
Swell the Strain	236
Swing those Gates ajar	7
Sunbeams	27
Sun of my Soul	249
Tell the Love of Jesus	70
Thanksgiving Hymn	217
Thanks be to God	150
Thanks to Thee, our Father	216
That Beautiful Home	158
The Anchor of Hope	172
The Ark of Salvation	114
The Armor of God	78
The Battle March	202
The Book of the New Year	252
The Border Line	95
The Bread of Life	55
The Children's Song	110
The Christian Soldier	82
The City of God	152
The Cleansing Fountain	81
The Cleansing Stream	90
The Father's Promises	92
The Gates of Life	48
The Glad New Year	250
The Gospel Feast	34
The Gospel's Triumph	196
The Great Physician	207
The Happy, Golden Shore	42
The Haven of Peace	54
The Herald Angels	223
The Hills of Amethyst	133
The Home beyond the Blue	75
The King's Business hath haste	104
The Lord's Prayer, (chant)	113
The Lord arose	243
The Lord will provide	121
The Love of Christ	203
The Master is risen	242
The Mighty to Save	58
The Ocean of God's Love	201
The Other Shore	148
The Race is on	46
There is Room for all	161

INDEX OF TITLES.

	PAGE		PAGE
The Sabbath School	94	Watching at the Door	151
The Sacred Stream	164	Waves of Love	6
The Saviour's Call	117	We are marching on	52
The Sheaf-Bearers	214	We'll not give up the Bible	190
The Song of Heaven	174	We sing Thy Praise to-day	188
The Starry Crown	10	What do the Bells say?	168
The Time for Action	127	What will they tell Jesus?	30
The Wonderful Story	234	Who is He in Light arrayed?	238
Thine, wholly Thine	39	Wholly the Lord's	37
This is the Day	33	Why should not we?	103
Trusting in the Ark	197	Wonderful Light of His Love	21
Very close to Thee	49	Working for Jesus	96
Victory will soon be won	84	Ye Soldiers of the Lord, arise	144
Watch and pray	180	Youthful Praise	97

INDEX OF FAMILIAR HYMNS.

	PAGE		PAGE
Abide with me! Fast falls the eventide	177	Jesus, Saviour, pilot me	65
A charge to keep I have	219	Just as I am, without one plea	141
Alas! and did my Saviour bleed?	163	Lead, kindly Light, amid th'encircling	143
All hail the power of Jesus name	50	Lord, I hear of show'rs of blessing	123
Blest be the tie that binds	61	Mary to the Saviour's tomb	227
Break Thou the bread of life	55	My faith looks up to Thee	137
Come, let us lift our joyful eyes	91	O day of rest and gladness	187
Come Thou Almighty King	57	Oh, for a heart to praise my God	215
Come, ye disconsolate	167	O think of a home over there	79
Come ye that love the Lord	145	Rock of Ages, cleft for me	47
Fade, fade, each earthly joy	135	Sowing in the morning, sowing seeds	169
Hark! ten thousand harps and voices	51	Stand up! stand up for Jesus!	63
Holy, Holy, Holy! Lord God Almighty	147	Sun of my soul Thou Saviour dear	249
I am coming to the cross	237	The great Physician now is near	207
I hear Thy welcome voice	71	The morning light is breaking	157
I love to steal awhile away	19	There is a fountain filled with blood	81
In the cross of Christ, I glory	67	What a friend we have in Jesus	179
Jesus, refuge of my soul	87	Work for the night is coming	73

INDEX OF SUBJECTS.

Anniversary.

	PAGE
Excelsior	166
Going out to Battle	136
'Neath the Banner glorious	32
Stand firm	126
The Armor of God	78
The Battle March	202
Victory will soon be won	84

Children's Day.
(See also Anniversary.)

	PAGE
Buds and Blossoms	100
Joyous Children's Day	101
Our Festal Day	208
The Children's Song	110
Why should not we?	103

Christmas.

	PAGE
Bethlehem's Star	231
Carol the Christmas Song	225
Christmas Bells	224
Christmas Bells are ringing	230
Christmas Music	233
Christmas Thoughts	222
Golden Bells	228
Ring out the Bells	226
The Wonderful Story	234

Devotional.
(See also Familiar Hymns.)

	PAGE
All for Jesus	131
Grace divine and free	35
Hide me, Saviour	25

INDEX OF SUBJECTS.

	PAGE
His Guiding Hand	111
Mercy's Free	153
Singing for Jesus	199
Save and comfort me	107
Thine, wholly Thine	39
Very close to Thee	49
Wonderful Light of His Love	21
Wholly the Lord's	37

Easter.

Christ is risen to-day	241
Easter Offerings	240
Glorious Easter Day	89
Hail the Risen King	239
Swell the Strain	236
The Lord arose	243
The Master is risen	242
Who is He in Light arrayed?	238

Encouragement and Cheer.

Better further on	142
Go tell it to Jesus	36
In Well-doing, be not weary	12
It all will be Bright	74
Just a little Sunshine	108
Let the Light shine in	17
Soldier of the Cross	159
The Starry Crown	10
We are marching on	52

Heaven.

Beyond the Gates	116
Gathering Home	18
That Beautiful Home	158
The Gates of Life	48
The Happy, Golden Shore	42
The Haven of Peace	54
The Home beyond the Blue	75
The other Shore	148

Invitation.

At the Pool of Siloam	80
Fount for Cleansing	20
Ho, every One that thirsteth	60
Is your Heart all cleansed?	77
Let the King come in	22
Only ask, believing	31
The Gospel Feast	34
This is the Day	33
What will they tell Jesus?	30

Missionary.

Help a Little	28
Reaping where thou hast not sown	16
Sow and Gather	98
Tell the Love of Jesus	70
The King's Business hath haste	104
The Gospel's Triumph	196

Occasional.

	PAGE
A happy New Year	248
Flag of America	189
For God and Country	245
Land of the Free	247
National Hymn	185
New Year Greeting	251
Our Native Land	246
Resting in the Sunlight (Funereal)	175
The Book of the New Year	252
The Hills of Amethyst (Funereal)	133
The Glad New Year	250

Praise and Thanksgiving.

Blessed is He that cometh	220
Crown Him forever	128
Crown Him Lord of all	50
Crowned with Praise	3
Harvest Thanksgiving	213
Light	64
Praise the Lord	218
Praise waiteth for Thee	212
Thanksgiving Hymn	217
Thanks to Thee, our Father	216
The City of God	152
The Mighty to Save	58
The Sheaf-Bearers	214

Temperance.

Battling for Temperance	105
God speed the Right	165
The Temperance Banner	139

Receiving the Saviour.

Let Thy Mercy Shine on me	183
The Ark of Salvation	114
The Cleansing Stream	90
Thine, wholly Thine	39
Watching at the Door	151
Wonderful Light of His Love	21

The Sabbath and Bible.

Call to Prayer	182
O Day of Rest	187
The Sabbath School	94
We'll not give up the Bible	190
What do the Bells say?	168

Work and Effort.

Always True	56
Be ready and obey	112
Be up and doing	62
Labor for the Master	40
Loyalty to the Master	66
Put on the whole Armor	72
Sow and Gather	98
Standing for the Good and Right	23
The Race is on	46
Working for Jesus	96

www.ingramcontent.com/pod-product-compliance
Lightning Source LLC
Chambersburg PA
CBHW021400230426
43666CB00006B/593

*9 7 8 3 3 3 7 2 7 0 4 4 5 *